Introduction To

COIN MAGIC

Shigeo Futagawa

Born in 1943 in Yokohama, Japan. Graduated from Keio University. Has taught mathematics at several High Schools. Manager of a private school teaching English and other subjects. His interest in the field of Magic began in his first year of high school. He was a member of the Keio University Magic Club and is now secretary of the Magic Maniacs Circle. In 1972 he toured the United States and Canada with Arnold Furst. He has contributed to many magic magazines in Japan and to the S.O.B., Jr. magazine published by Lloyd Jones.

Introduction To

COIN MAGIC

By
Shigeo Futagawa

BORDEN PUBLISHING COMPANY
ALHAMBRA, CALIFORNIA

Translation from Japanese by Roy Matsumura
Japan Printing Co.
Gardena, California

Drawings by Shigeo Futagawa
Artwork by Robert A. Wagner
English edition produced by Arnold Furst

ISBN 0-91526-23-7

Dedication To

Shigeo Takagi

Born in Tokyo in 1930 and began to study magic when seven years old. Today, Shigeo Takagi is head of the Research Department of the Library of Congress of Japan. He is now the President of the S.A.M. assembly of Japan and also President of the Magic Maniacs Circle and Tokyo Cardician's Club and Vice-president of Japan Magician's Association.

Shigeo Takagi has written over sixty books on magic and kindred subjects and is the originator of many coin effects. He appears often on television programs and devotes much of his time to lecturing for magic clubs and conventions.

Table of Contents

Forward

In JAPAN the interest in the field of Magic stems from the days of Ten Ichi and Tenkatsu. With the advent of television, the magician has been able to come into the home and reach many more millions than before. In the theatres and cabarets the magician has the advantage of assistants and large pieces of apparatus.

When performing close-up magic, the performer uses small easily recognized objects and gives the appearance of great skill since the tricks are performed with only the use of his two hands.

Coin magic offers a great many opportunities to the young performer as there is a minimum expense for the articles used and very often the coins can be borrowed for the particular performance. Those in the audience will recognize the coins used and accept the idea that these coins are of a solid substance and ordinarily will not pass thru such material as a cloth handkerchief or drinking glass.

The ability to handle the coins and manipulate them for the magical effects is a skill which until recently was acquired only by instructions from a professional coin magician.

Today instruction from leading coin magicians like Dai Vernon and Slydini will cost upwards to $60.00 an hour. I was fortunate to have received instruction in this skill from Shigeo Takagi who has been both my teacher and friend since my University days. He urged me to write this book and I took great pains with the drawings and explanations as I want to pass on to the reader much of the understanding of this subject which I have received over the years from Mr. Takagi and also from The Great Tenkai.

This book contains most careful and detailed instructions for the basic moves and techniques of coin magic and I wish to remind the reader that when one wishes to acquire a new skill, one must use that skill over and over. That is called practice and in this book you will find many pages of practice for first one hand and then the other and then for both hands. As you practice over and over you will be able to perform the techniques in a natural manner and I feel sure you will delight in seeing your friends puzzled by the tricks in your repetoire.

As I traveled around the world in 1972 I found amateur and professional magicians everywhere interested in meeting me and showing me their tricks. I have found magicians to be welcomed everywhere and the performance of coin tricks can be easily understood to the extent that it might be considered as an "international and universal language."

Please take the time to learn each trick well. Your ability to perform Coin Magic will provide you and your friends much enjoyment on many occasions.

Shigeo Futagawa

Chapter 1

The Close Up Mat

Most of the coin techniques and effects described in this book can be performed with coins the size of an American Quarter. In some of the tricks a handkerchief or drinking glass is also used. In each instance, these articles are ordinary and un-prepared.

The close up mat is perhaps the only piece of special

equipment that the student of Coin Magic will need to acquire. The mat can be a small carpet or household rug which can be purchased in some stores like Woolworth or Grant or K-mart.

The size of the mat will vary with each performer. The large size will be approximately 18" by 30". The smaller pads are about 11" by 16" and are often preferred as they can be carried about more easily in the performer's case.

The most important feature of the close up mat is that it provides the magician with a soft surface to perform and enables him to pick up the coins easily. Many Joke stores and magical supplies companies advertise close up mats made with a sheet of foam rubber inside a cloth covering.

When choosing a close up mat consideration should be given to the color. White or some light color should be avoided as these mats become soiled easily. Red or blue are unsuited since when playing cards or poker chips are placed upon them, they sometimes blend with the colors. For this same reason, close up mats with a pattern are unsatisfactory. The most popular colors for the close up mat is green or black. They provide a good contrasting background for the coins.

Chapter 2

Tricks Without Sleights

HANDKERCHIEF AND COIN

EFFECT: A handkerchief is draped over the right hand. A coin is held thru the handkerchief which is then pulled away without disturbing the coin.

1. You will need a coin and one handkerchief. The handkerchief is shown as in this drawing.

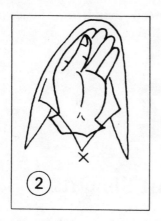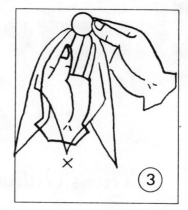

2. The right hand, which had been holding corner " X", now drapes the handkerchief over the extended fingers of the left hand. The corner "X" is dropped so that it is the corner nearest to the performer's body and it hangs about as low as the left wrist.

3. Turn the left hand to show the audience that the entire hand is covered. The right hand then picks up the coin and places it against the finger tips of the left hand which is still under the handkerchief. The folded edge of the handkerchief is now clipped between the right forefinger and the coin.

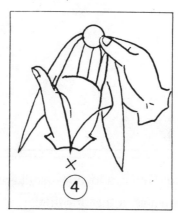

4. The left thumb is separated from the left forefinger and the thumb is brought towards the performer's body so that it is no longer under the handkerchief and it is hidden from the audience.

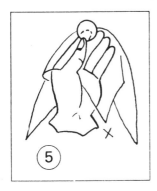

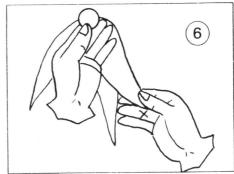

5. Left thumb now presses the coin against the left fingers which are still under the handkerchief and the right hand is withdrawn. The audience thinks that the coin is grasped in the center of the handkerchief.
6. The right hand now holds the handkerchief at corner "X" and the handkerchief is slowly withdrawn to the right.

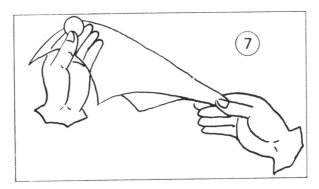

7. As the handkerchief is pulled away, the audience can see that the coin still remains in place.

COIN THRU BOTTOM OF GLASS

EFFECT: The coin is hit against the bottom of the glass and it is caused to pass into the glass.

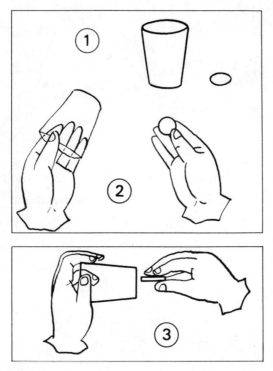

1. The glass and coin is placed on the table.
2. The glass is held in the left hand and the coin is in the right hand, as illustrated.
3. The bottom of the glass is facing the performer's right side. The coin is hit against the bottom of the glass several times so that the audience can hear the sound. You do not need to hit the glass very hard or rapidly. A deliberate tap is better.

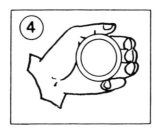

4. The glass is held in the left hand as this illustration shows. This drawing shows the performer's view of the left hand. The glass is actually held by the left thumb and little finger. There is an open space of about half an inch between the edge of the glass and the palm of the hand. The three other fingers rest lightly against the outside of the glass.

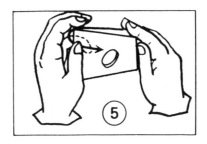

5. When the coin is hit against the bottom of the glass for the third time, the right hand moves a little bit forward and the coin is thrown in front of the glass so that it is caught by the three fingers of the left hand and it is allowed to drop into the glass after it has entered the left palm. Actually, the coin does not hit the bottom of the glass the third time. The right hand hits against the bottom of the glass as the coin is released.

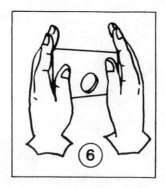

6. After the coin has entered the glass, the two hands grasp the glass as illustrated and then the audience can see that the coin is actually inside the glass. The coin you use may be a quarter or half a dollar.

RING AND COIN FREED FROM HANDKERCHIEF

EFFECT: A coin is placed in the center of a handkerchief and the four corners of that handkerchief are threaded thru a small ring. The coin and ring are removed from the handkerchief which a spectator thinks is securely containing them.

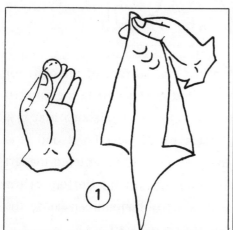

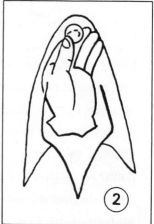

18

1. The performer uses a large white handkerchief, a borrowed finger ring and a coin which is too large to pass thru the ring. The performer holds the handkerchief with his right hand and the coin with the fingers of the left hand as illustrated.

2. The handkerchief is draped over the entire left hand which is holding the coin.

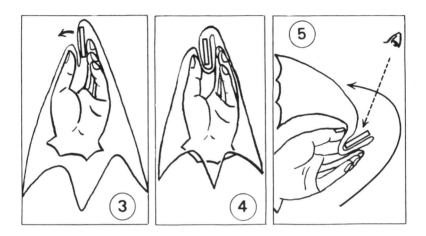

3. The right hand grasps the coin thru the handkerchief with the right thumb and forefinger. The left thumb is then removed slightly to allow the right thumb to push a portion of the handkerchief down between the left thumb and the coin.

4. With the right forefinger, the top of the coin is pushed back towards the performer's body. The entire coin is now rotated within the folds of the handkerchief so that it is wrapped as shown in this drawing.

5. The left thumb and fingers are extended towards the audience and the corner of the handkerchief closest to the audience is lifted to show the coin.

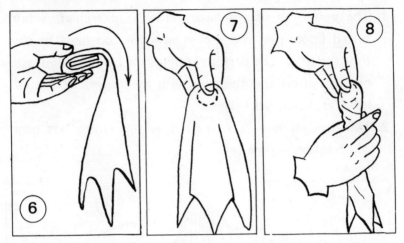

6. Drop the left arm and this causes the entire handkerchief to hang down from the left hand. The coin is now actually outside the handkerchief but it still appears to be inside.

7. Swing the body a bit to the left to hide the coin from the audience.

8. With his right hand, the performer now twists the handkerchief several times around the coin.

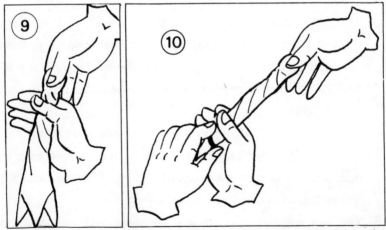

9. A spectator is asked to hold the coin which is within the twisted handkerchief. He is asked to hold tightly.

10. The performer slides his right hand down to the four corners of the handkerchief and since the left hand is now
free, it is used to pick up the borrowed finger ring and the
four corners of the handkerchief are threaded thru the
ring.

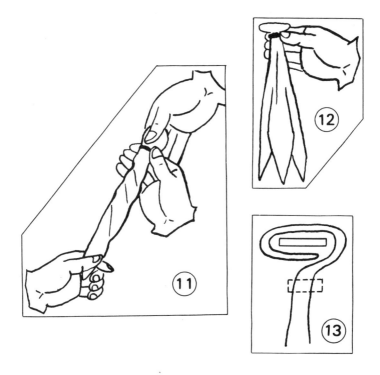

11. The left hand now grasps the four corners of the handkerchief which is threaded thru the ring and the right
hand slides the ring up towards the coin. The ring is
brought up tightly against the coin.

12. The spectator is asked to release his hold on the coin.

13. This shows the actual position of the coin which appears
to be wrapped in the handkerchief.

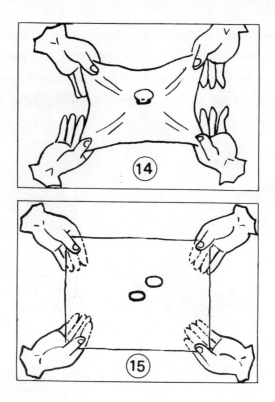

14. Two spectators from the audience are now asked to hold the four corners of the handkerchief as shown in this drawing. The handkerchief is thus extended with the ring in the middle and the coin apparently wrapped in the handkerchief within the ring. The handkerchief is held horizontal and level with the floor.

15. The performer new cups his two hands around the ring and coin and he removes the coin from within the folds of the handkerchief. First the coin is shown to the audience while the two hands are cupped around the ring. Secondly the ring is shown to the audience and now the ring and coin are both placed on the outstretched handkerchief as in this drawing.

Chapter 3

The Finger Palm

The finger palm is one of the most necessary techniques of coin magic. In this case, the fingers are used to hide the coin.

When performed properly, the spectators think the hand is empty when the coin is finger palmed and there are so many effects where it is necessary that they do think this.

When a coin is produced from the finger palm, the audience thinks that the coin came from the air. When a coin is vanished by the use of a finger palm, the audience thinks the coin has dissolved and can no longer be in the performer's hand. It is very important for you to learn this technique.

EXERCISE NO. 1. Learn how your hand looks when it is holding a coin and when it is empty.

1. Sit in front of a table. Relax. Drop your two hands on the table and study how the backs of the two empty hands appear.

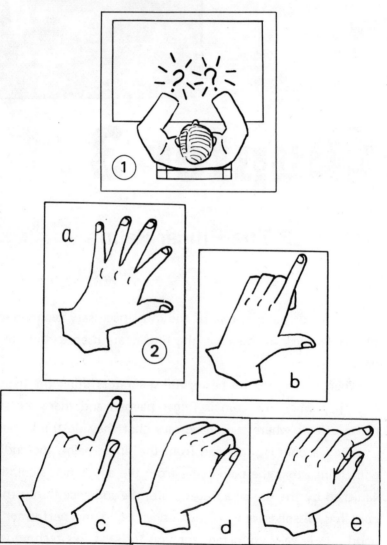

2. Here we have five possible positions you might see. We see muscular tension in all the five fingers of "a". We see strain in the thumb of "b". There is tension in the forefinger of "c" and the other fingers seem strained as well. Good examples of a relaxed position of an empty hand are shown in "d" and "e". The best position for our purpose is "e".

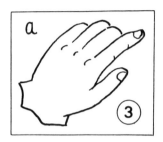

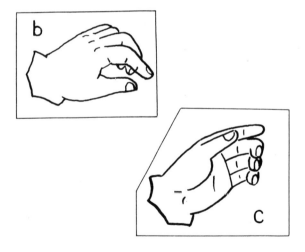

3. Imitate the position shown in these three drawings. The top view is "a". Side view is "b" and "c" is how the hand would appear if we could see it from up thru a glass top table. The hand is held without any spaces between the fingers.

EXERCISE NO. 2. Practise holding a half dollar.

 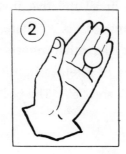 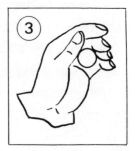

1. The left hand is resting on the table with the palm up.
2. Put the coin on the ring finger, at the second joint.
3. Relax the three fingers and hold them so there is no space
   between them. Slowly bend the three fingers so that they
   curl around the coin to the extent that if the hand is
   turned over, the coin will not fall.

EXCERCISE NO. 3. Practise holding a small coin.

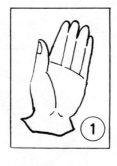 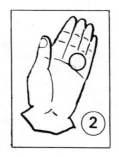

1. Left hand is rested palm up on the table.
2. Put small coin on the base of the ring finger.
3. The three small fingers curl around the coin.
4. This shows the small coin being held by the middle finger.

EXERCISE NO. 4. Practise the finger palm using only one hand.

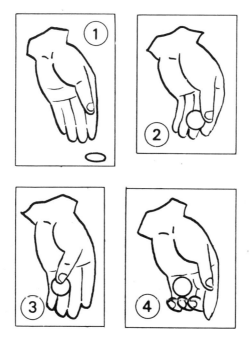

1. Coin is on the table.
2. Pick up coin.
3. Use the thumb to pull coin up to the finger palm position.
4. The three smallest fingers are bent and they hold the coin without using the thumb or forefinger. The thumb must be relaxed.

EXERCISE NO. 5. Producing a coin from the finger palm.

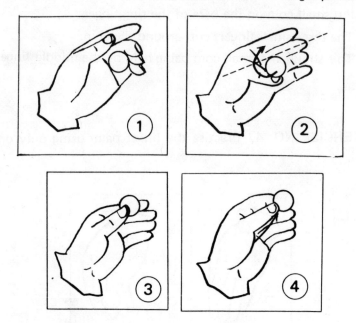

1. Shows coin in finger palm position.
2. Left thumb goes under the coin.
3. Thumb pushed the coin up and it is turned over. It looks to the audience like the coin was produced from the air.
4. The coin is pushed still further up until it is at the very tips of the fingers and thumb. This gives a much better view of the entire coin. As the coin is pushed to the finger tips, it is best to curl in the three small fingers.

COIN INTO PANTS POCKET

EFFECT: A coin seems to pass thru the cloth of the pants and into the pocket.

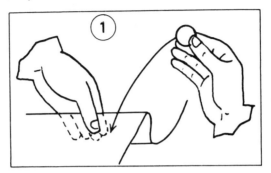

1. The coin is shown in the right hand and the left hand catches a small amount of the cloth. About an inch or so is grasped. The grasped cloth is at the pocket area of the pants leg.

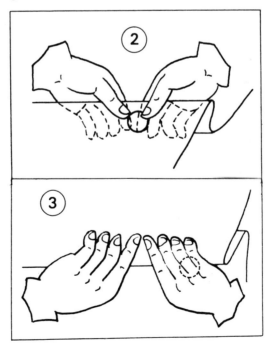

2. Put the coin on top of the cloth and both the right and left thumbs press down on the coin.

3. Both hands turn the cloth up and as soon as the coin is hidden from view, the right hand pulls the coin up into the finger palm position.

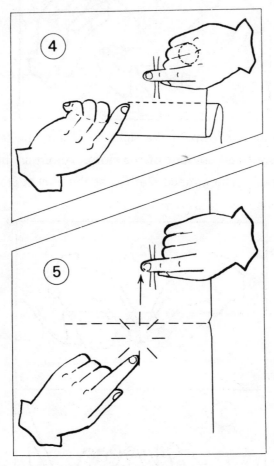

4. The left forefinger presses down and the right hand is removed from under the cloth. The right hand drops about three inches and catches the cloth with the thumb and forefinger.

5. The right hand pulls the cloth down until the cloth is now straight and the area under the left forefinger is now clear. The coin has vanished.

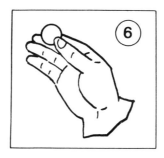

6. The right hand goes into the right pants pocket and the coin from the finger palm is brought to the finger tips as it is produced from the pocket.

It is possible to improve this effect by first having a duplicate coin inside the right pants pocket. When the coin is first put on the cloth (drawing No. 2) this coin is put on top of the coin which is inside the pocket and it is therefore under the cloth which is grasped and turned over. (drawing No. 3) After the coin has been finger palmed and the cloth pulled to show the coin has vanished (drawing No. 5) it is possible to invite someone from the audience to reach into the pants pocket and remove the coin.

VANISHING COIN

EFFECT: Coin held by the elbow is vanished.

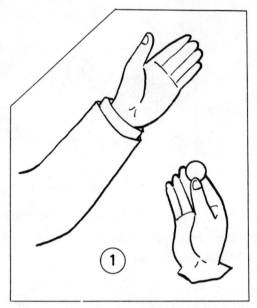

1. Performer should wear a coat or jacket. The coin is shown at the fingertips of the right hand. The left hand is outstretched as pictured.

2. The coin is pressed by the thumb into the inside area near the left elbow. The other four fingers of the right hand grasp the coin thru the coat material.

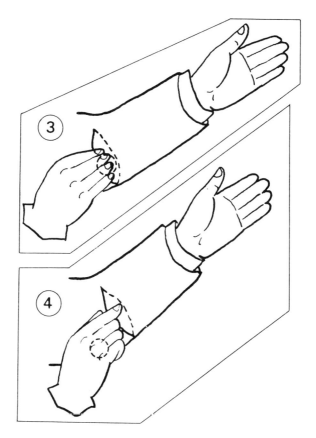

3. The right hand now turns over and hides the coin from view.
4. The right thumb now pulls the hidden coin out from the folds of the coat material and into the finger palm. The right forefinger continues to press down into the spot where the coin had been originally placed.

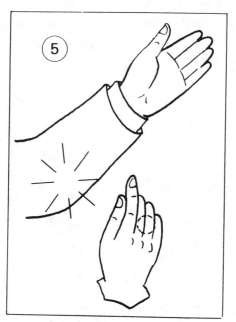

5. The right thumb is removed from under the folds of the coat sleeve and the left arm is extended so the audience can see that the coin has vanished.

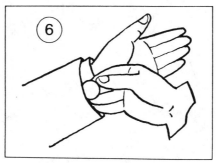

6. The right hand goes into the left sleeve with the finger tips and the performer explains that the coin went thru the material and is now in the sleeve. At the same time, the coin is brought from the finger palm to the finger tips and it is at this time allowed to drop into the left sleeve.

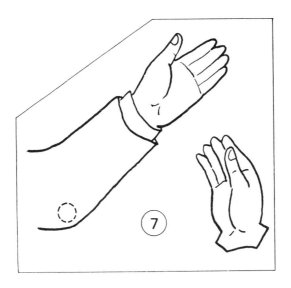

7. At this point the right hand is kept closed after the coin is dropped down the left sleeve.

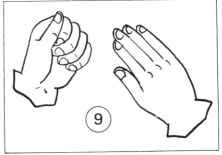

8. The left hand is opened and the closed right hand is brought to the left hand as though the coin is in the right hand.

9. The performer acts as though he is now holding the coin in his left hand.

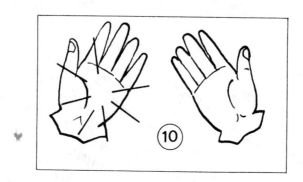

10. The performer says a magic word and then opens first the right hand and then the left hand and both are shown empty. The performer can conclude this effect by inviting a member of the audience to come up and feel the coin which is now resting inside the left sleeve.

TWO EXCELLENT BOOKS

"COIN MAGIC" by Jean Hugard was published in 1972 by Louis Tannen. It has a wealth of information on coin tricks and manipulation, clearly explained with many illustration.

"MODERN COIN MAGIC" by J.B. Boby was written in 1952 and several revised editions have been published by Magic, Inc. of Chicago, Illinois. This 520 page book is one of the most complete over written on this subject.

Chapter 4

The Coin Vanish

This is another important technique of coin magic and these exercises should be practised many times in front of a mirror.

EXERCISE NO. 1. Holding the coin.

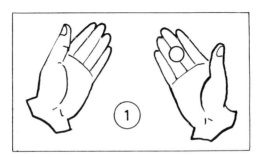

1. Coin is placed on the fingers of the right hand and the left hand is also held with the palm up.

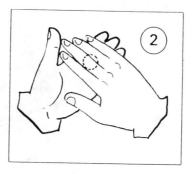

2. Coin is put into left hand.

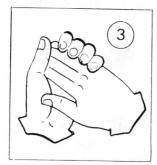 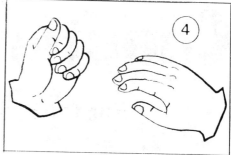

3. The four fingers of the left hand close by curling around the right hand.

4. The right hand is removed as the left fingers close into fist.

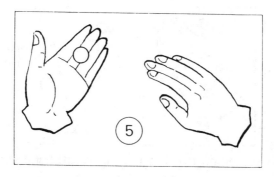

5. The left hand is then opened and we see the coin.

EXERCISE NO. 2. Finger clip.

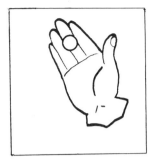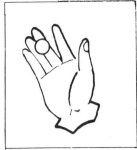

1. The right hand is held open with the coin resting on the middle finger with about ¼ of an inch extending over the forefinger and the ring finger.

2. Separate the forefinger a little bit from the other three fingers.

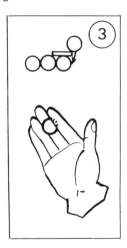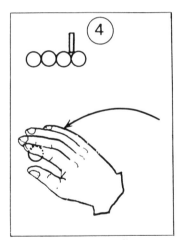

3. The forefinger is brought down on top of the coin so that it is "clipped" between the two fingers, but the coin should not be visable from the back of the hand.

4. The movement of the forefinger is not seen by the audience as it is covered by the movement of the hand as it is turned palm down and moved to the left.

EXERCISE NO. 3. Change coin from Finger Clip to Finger Palm

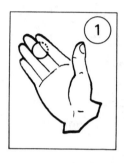 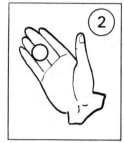 

1. Coin is now in between forefinger and middle finger. The hand is held in front of performer, with the small finger at the bottom of hand and the palm is facing the performer.
2. The forefinger is taken away from the coin and that causes the coin to fall on top of the two middle fingers.
3. The coin is now in position for the finger palm, so the thumb is put on the coin and pulls it into position for the finger palm.

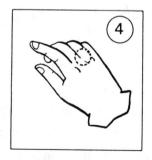

4. Relax the right hand into a natural position.

EXERCISE NO. 4. Vanishing the coin.

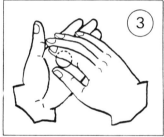

1. Coin is on the center fingers of the right hand and the left hand is turned palm up. The right hand is moved towards the left hand and then turned over.

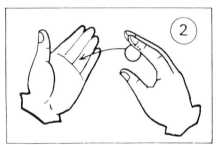

2. The right hand then does the moves explained above for the ' finger clip" The coin is here shown in the "finger clip".
3. This time the right forefinger is not relaxed and so the coin remains in the 'finger clip".

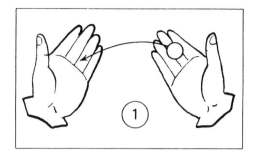

4. The left hand closes around the right fingers as though it is holding the coin.

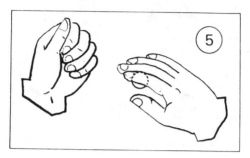

5. The left hand moves forward as though to take the coin. The right hand does not move as the left hand moves away and the performer directs his attention towards the left hand. This should cause the audience to look at the left hand, also. The performer must keep the fingers of his left hand a bit loose to give the appearance of actually holding a coin. A shows the fingers clenched too tightly. This is incorrect. B shows the proper way for the fingers to appear.

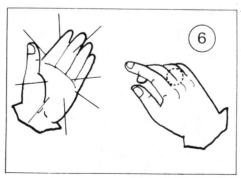

6. Open the left hand to show the coin has vanished. At this time the right hand goes into Exercise No. 3 which puts the coin from the "finger clip" into the finger palm.

COINS ACROSS

EFFECT: One coin joins another coin across the table as the performer slowly counts from "one" to "ten". You will need just the two coins for this effect.

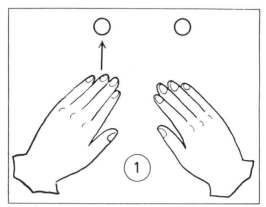

1. At the start of this effect the two coins are resting on the table about eight inches apart. The two hands are rested on the table, palms down.

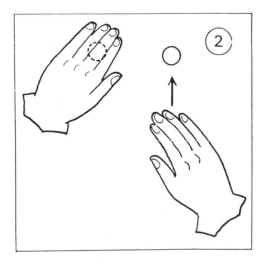

2. The left hand covers the coin on the left side of the table and performer says, "One".

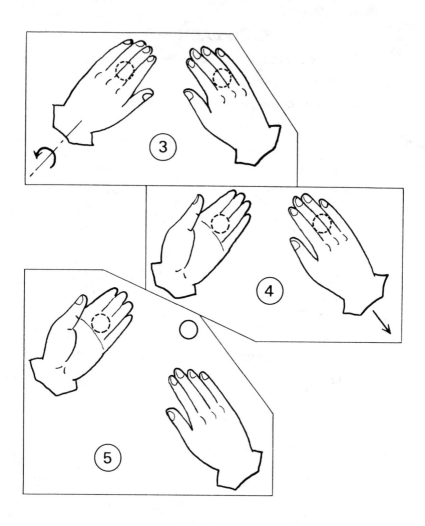

3. The right hand covers the coin on the right side of the table and performer says, "Two".

4. The left hand is then turned face up with the back of the hand resting on the coin as the performer counts, "Three"

5. The right hand then is withdrawn from the coin and the performer says, "Four".

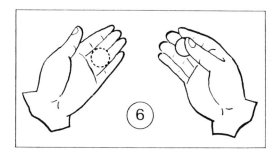

6. The performer then picks up the exposed coin and counts, "Five".

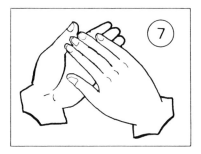

7. The magician acts as though he is putting this coin into the palm of the left hand. The coin is actually finger clipped and the left hand is closed to give the appearance of receiving the coin.

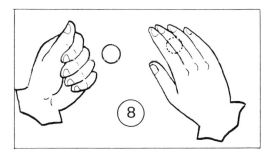

8. The left hand is now closed into a fist and the right hand is removed. As the left fist is formed the audience can see the coin which had been under the left hand. The per-

former counts, "Six". At this time the performer changes the coin in his right hand from the finger clip to the finger palm.

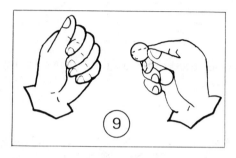

9. The right hand now picks up the coin which is remaining on the table, with his right thumb and forefinger and it is slowly brought into the right fist as the performer counts, "Seven".

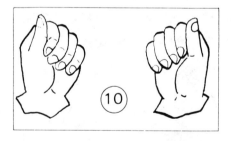

10. The two closed fists are moved slowly up and down for effect and the right fist is relaxed slightly to allow the two coins to strike against each other as the performer says, "Eight". You should practice dropping the second coin on to the coin which is finger palmed so that the sound will be most pronounced.

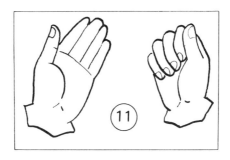

11. The left hand is opened and shown to be empty as the magician counts, 'Nine".

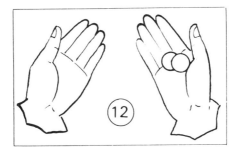

12. The right hand is opened, showing the two coins as the magician says, "Ten".

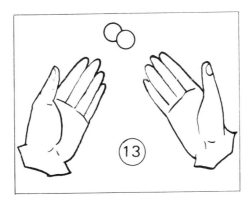

13. The two coins are then dropped on to the table in front of the two empty hands.

COIN AND FOUNTAIN PEN ROUTINE

EFFECT: The two hands are shown to be empty. A coin suddenly appears in the left hand and then is caused to vanish when that hand is tapped by a fountain pen. The performer explains that he is using a "magic pen". The fountain pen is put into an inside coat pocket. The left hand then appears to catch something from the air and this is put into the right hand. Suddenly the fountain pen appears in the left hand and it is used to tap the right hand which is opened to show it is holding the coin.

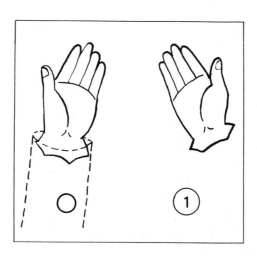

1. One coin is hidden in the left sleeve. The fountain pen is clipped to the inside coat pocket. Both hands are bent at the elbow as they are shown to be empty.

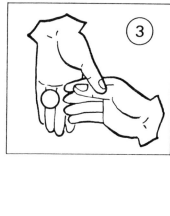

2. The left arm is allowed to drop down as the right hand is stretched out and appears to be catching something from the air. At the same time, the coin hidden in the left sleeve is allowed to fall into the half opened left hand.

3. The back of the left hand is towards the audience and so they do not see the palmed coin. The right hand then appears to be putting someting (which was caught from the thin air) into the left hand and the left hand closes.

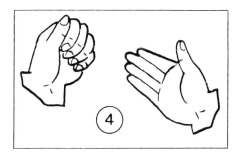

4. The right hand is then opened and seen to be empty while the left hand remains closed.

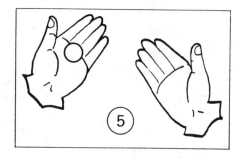

5. The left hand is now opened to reveal the coin.

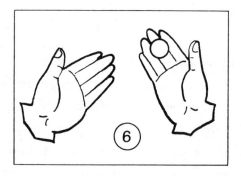

6. The coin is now transferred to the right hand.

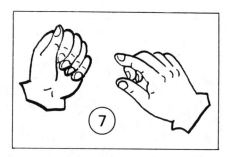

7. The coin is now finger palmed in the right hand as the performer acts as though he is putting the coin back into the left hand.

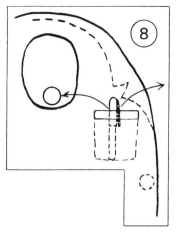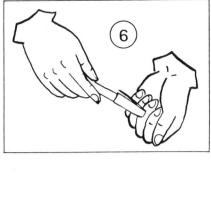

8. The right hand now goes inside the coat to withdraw the fountain pen. However, first of all, the finger palmed coin in the right hand is now dropped down the left sleeve. Then the performer withdraws the fountain pen from his inside coat pocket.

9. The fountain pen is then used to tap against the back of the left fist.

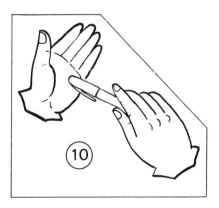

10. The left hand is opened to show the coin has vanished.

11. The left hand is dropped as before and the performer now returns the fountain pen back inside his coat. However, instead of putting it into the inside pocket, the pen is now dropped down the left sleeve.

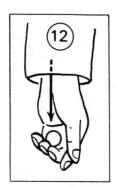

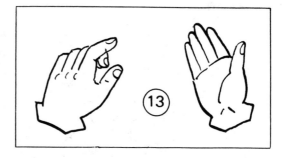

12. At the same time as the fountain pen was going inside the coat, the left hand was dropped down and the coin was received into the left hand. As soon as the performer has the coin in his left hand, the left arm is bent to prevent the fountain pen from falling.

13. The right hand is shown empty.

14. The left hand acts as though something is being caught in the air.

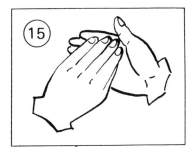

15. At this point the coin is actually transferred into the right hand.

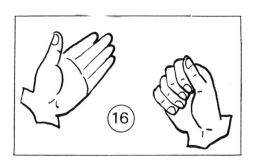

16. The left hand is opened to show it is empty.

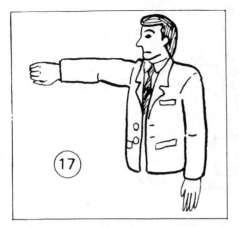

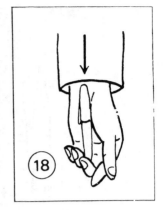

17. The left hand is then dropped on the left side which is away from the audience as the performer raises his right hand and looks at it.

18. The fountain pen is now allowed to drop into the left hand.

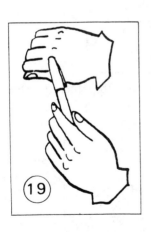

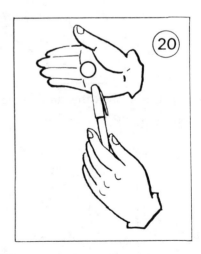

19. The left hand is extended with the fountain pen which is tapped against the back of the right hand.

20. The right hand is opened to show the coin.

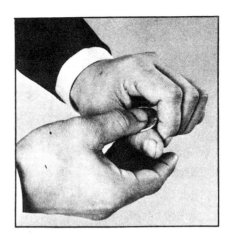

Chapter 5

The Tunnel Vanish

EFFECT: The simple vanish of a coin.

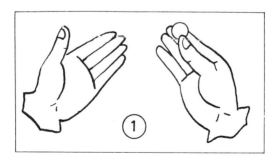

1. The coin is held at the fingertips of the forefinger, middle finger and thumb of the right hand.

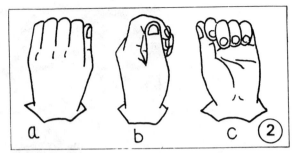

2. The left hand is formed into a loose fist with the thumb and forefinger touching lightly. This picture shows three views of the left hand so you will see that the fist is open at the bottom.

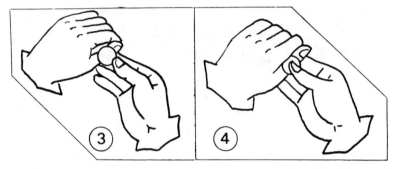

3. The right hand brings the coin up to the left fist and rests the coin on top of the left thumb.

4. The right thumb presses the coin down on the left thumb as the fingers of the right hand go under the left first.

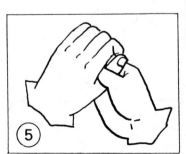
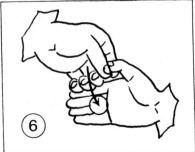

5. The coin is pushed into the bottomless left fist and then it drops into the right fingers.

6. As soon as the coin is dropped into the open right hand, the performer finger palms the coin. The picture shows the two hands apart for the benefit of the reader. When doing this effect the hands are actually much closer together.

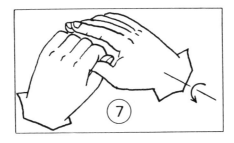

7. As soon as the coin is finger palmed, the right hand is turned so that the back of the right fingers are uppermost and the thumb is then removed.

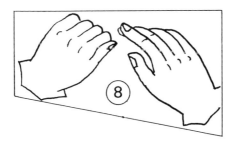

8. At the same time, the left fingers close upon the imaginary coin. The left fist is closed now and is no longer bottomless.

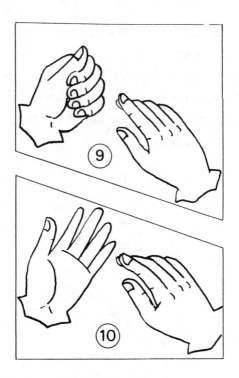

9. The left fist is turned so that the audience and performer can look at it.

10. The left hand is then opened to show the coin has vanished.

DOLLAR CHANGED INTO FOUR QUARTERS

EFFECT: The dollar bill is folded into a small packet and put into the left fist. When opened, the fist contains four quarters.

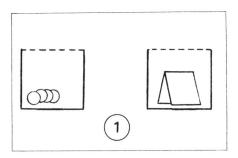

1. Four quarters are in the left coat pocket and the dollar bill is in the right coat pocket.

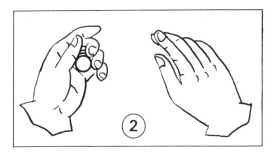

2. The hands are seen to be empty as the performer reaches into his right coat pocket to withdraw the dollar bill and at the same time, he reaches into his left coat pocket and finger palms the four quarters. The performer explains that this represents a problem he once had in a situation where he needed some coins and could only find a dollar bill in his pockets. The four quarters are in the finger palm position of his left hand and therefore the audience is not aware that he has anything in that hand.

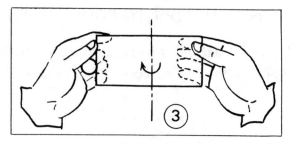

3. The dollar bill which had been removed from the right pocket is stretched out for the audience to see.

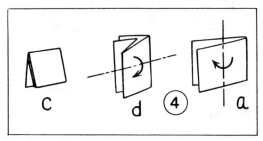

4. The dollar bill is folded in half (a) and then into fourths (b) and then into eighths (c).

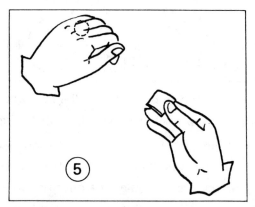

5. The left hand is now formed into a loose bottomless fist as necessary for the tunnel vanish and the performer explains that the left fist will serve as a "change making machine".

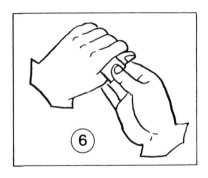 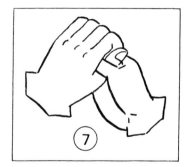

6. The folded bill is put on top of the left thumb and pressed by the right thumb and pushed into the bottom-less fist.

7. Since it is more difficult to get the folded bill to drop, it is best to use the right thumb to push the bill down into the right fingers so that they can finger palm the bill at that time.

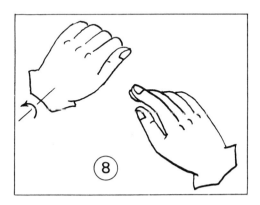

8. The left hand is withdrawn from the right hand and then the left fist is closed tightly and the fist is turned up as in the next drawing.

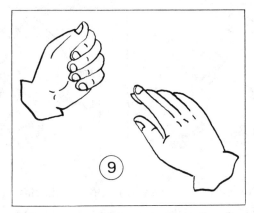

9. The left fist is now turned up so that the fingertips are uppermost and the performer and audience look at that hand.

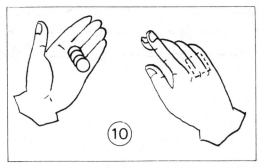

10. The left hand is now opened to show the four quarters.

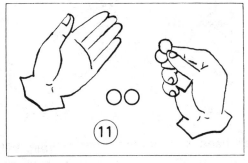

11. Put two quarters on the table and retain two of the quarters in the right hand.

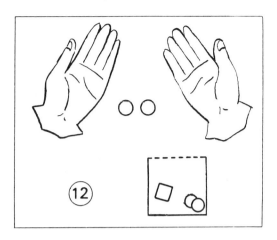

12. Performer now puts the two remaining quarters into his right coat pocket and at that time he leaves the folded dollar bill.

COINS ACROSS (Version No. 2)

EFFECT: Performer has two coins, one in each hand. The hands are closed and when opened, both coins are in the right hand. No need to be at a table for this version. Performer may be standing or sitting.

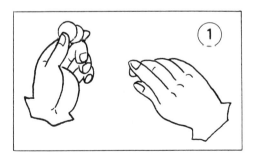

1. Performer takes two coins out of his pocket. They are held in the left hand and are shown to the audience.

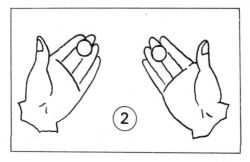

2. Now one coin is put on top of the fingers of each hand.

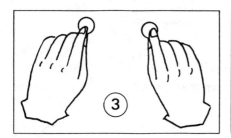

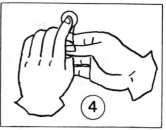

3. The thumb and forefinger of each hand now holds a single coin. The other fingers are closed into a lightly held fist and the backs of each hand is upward.

4. The right hand coin is now placed on top of the left thumb and the coin is then pushed into the left fist.

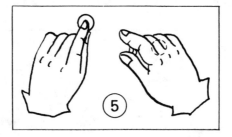

5. The performer does the tunnel vanish with this coin and the coin ends up in the finger palm of the right hand. The right hand is then turned with the back upward and the right hand is withdrawn.

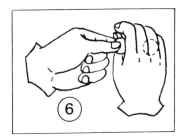 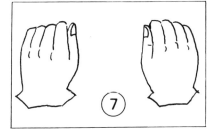

6. The left hand fingers are now closed into a tight fist while the coin is still held by the thumb and forefinger. The left fist is turned so that the back of the hand is turned down and the right hand is formed into a fist. The coin held by the left hand is now pushed into the right fist. Care should be taken at this time that the two coins do not hit or touch as they must be prevented from making any noise. Keep the first coin near the little finger.

7. Both hands are now tightly clenched and turned with their backs upwards.

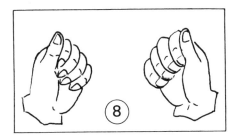

8. Both fists are raised slightly and then turned over. The fingers are unclenched slightly and the two coins in the right hand are allowed to hit together for a clicking sound.

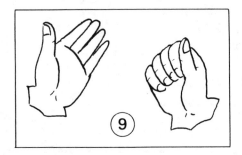

9. The left hand is now opened so the audience can see the coin has vanished from that hand.

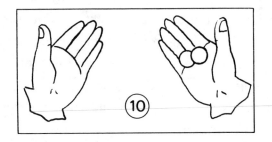

10. The right hand is opened for the audience to see both coins.

Chapter
6

The Thumb Palm

This is another important technique used in many coin tricks. In this technique the coin is hidden by the use of the thumb.

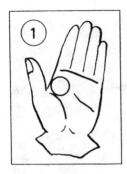
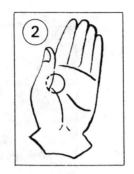

EXERCISE NO. 1. Holding the coin under the thumb.

1. Left hand is held with the palm up. The coin is placed at the base of the forefinger and the base of the thumb.

2. The palm is held very flat and the thumb is brought close to the palm so that the coin is caught under the thumb. The coin should be deep under the fleshy part of the thumb; down into the "v" of the thumb.

3. The left hand is turned over so that the back of the hand is upward and the fingers relax so that it does not appear that anything is held in that hand.

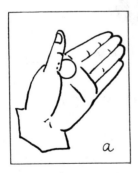

The most common errors in this technique is that either the thumb is held so stiff that (a) it sticks up in a pronounced position or else (b) the thumb is curled too far into the left palm. Both extremes must be avoided.

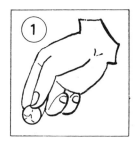 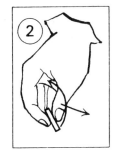 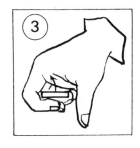

EXERCISE NO. 2. Using one hand for the thumb palm.

Part A

1. The right hand is held with the fingers pointing down and the coin is held by the thumb and forefinger and middle finger.

2. The coin is clipped between the forefinger and the middle finger and the thumb is removed.

3. These two fingers are curled upward.

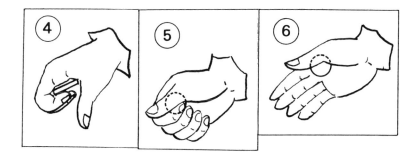

4. As the fingers bend upwards, the coin is turned sideways.

5. The coin is then pressed under the thumb.

6. The four fingers are now opened and the coin is held entirely by the thumb.

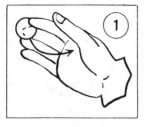 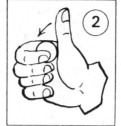 

Part B

1. The coin is held between the tips of the first two fingers. The hand is outstretched, but the fingers are not pointing down.
2. All four fingers curl into a loose fist.
3. The thumb presses down on the coin.

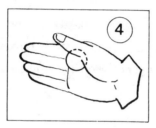

4. The fingers now open, leaving the coin under the thumb.

EXERCISE NO. 3. Producing the coin from the thumb palm.

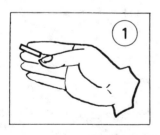 

1. The coin is clipped between the tips of the first two fingers. The thumb goes under the coin.
2. Thumb pushed the coin up and it makes it's appearance.

EXERCISE NO. 4. Vanishing the coin.

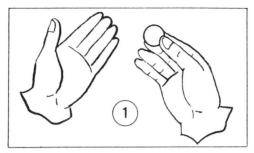

Part A

1. The coin is held at the tips of the fingers of the right hand and is shown as the hand is held palm up.

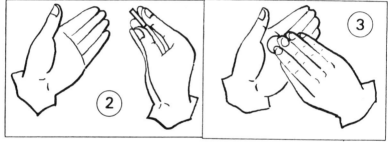

2. The right hand moves towards the open left hand and the back of the right hand turns up.

3. In this picture the right hand has just reached the left hand.

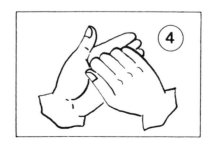

4. Here the right hand puts the coin into the thumb palm, using the moves described in EXERCISE NO. 2, Part A.

 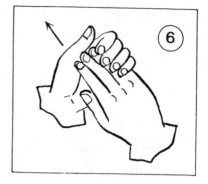

5. The four fingers of the right hand are now outstretched, the thumb is pressed tightly against the forefinger and holding the coin.

6. We must explain that in pictures #3 and #4 and #5 it appears that the left hand is open with the fingers extended. Actually, the left fingers are bent slightly so that they cover the action of the right fingers putting the coin into the thumb palm.

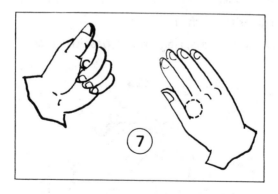

7. The right hand fingers are outstretched and does not move as the left fist is raised slightly. Performer looks at his left fist.

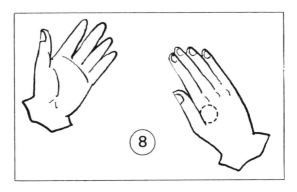

8. Performer blows at the left fist as the right hand is slowly dropped. The left hand is opened to show the coin has vanished.

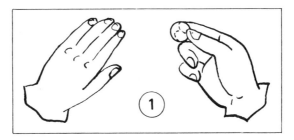

Part B

1. Coin is held in right hand. The left hand is held palm down.

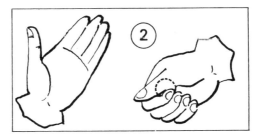

2. Performer looks at the left hand which is now turned palm up. Mention is made of the left hand and that should direct the audience's attention to it. At the same

time the right hand is lowered and the coin in held in the thumb palm.

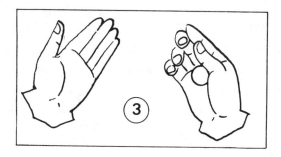

3. Performer acts like the the coin in held in his right finger tips.

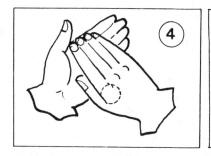 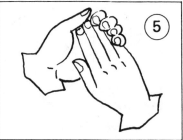

4. Right hand is brought quickly over the left palm.
5. The left hand closes around the fingers of right hand.

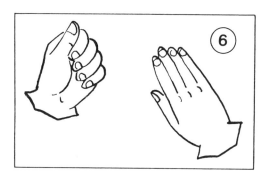

6. The left fist is brought slightly forward and the right hand is kept still.

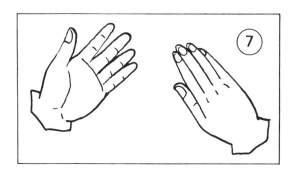

7. Performer says a few magic words as he opens left hand.

TRICK COINS FOR THE MAGICIAN

The reader of this book can obtain a catalog of Trick Coins (Copper/Silver coins, two-headed coins, folding coins, etc.) by sending a stamped, self-addressed envelope to Bob Wagner, 114 South Croft Avenue, Los Angeles, Cal. 90048

COIN VANISH

EFFECT: A coin is put into the left hand and vanished. Both hands are then shown to be empty.

Method No. 1. Using the outside breast pocket of coat.

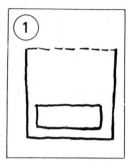

1. This drawing is to show the outside breast pocket of the performer's coat and a small handkerchief is rolled up and pushed into the bottom of that pocket in order to keep that pocket open.

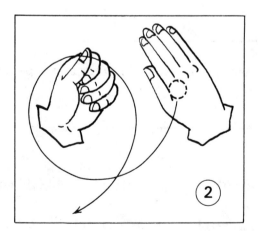

2. A coin is held in the right hand and in the act of placing the coin into the left hand, the coin is thumb palmed in

the right hand. The performer acts like the left hand is holding the coin and he moves his right hand in the manner of making a "magic pass" and so that hand moves in the direction indicated by the arrow in this picture.

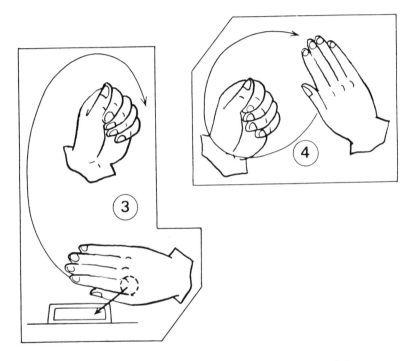

3. At the second turn of the "magic pass", the right hand goes close to the top of the breast pocket and the coin is dropped into the open pocket. This picture is a "top view" of the two hands as the right hand comes over the breast pocket.

4. Having dropped the coin into the breast pocket, the performer continues with his "magic pass" but now each circle comes closer to the left fist.

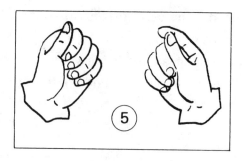

5. Suddenly the "magic pass" stops and the right hand fingers snap.

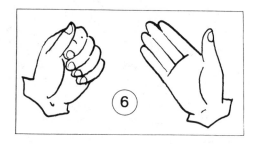

6. The right hand is opened to show it is empty.

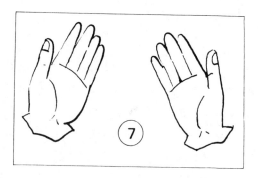

7. The left hand is also opened to show the coin has vanished.

Method No. 2. Also using outside breast pocket of coat.

1. As in the first method, the handkerchief is rolled up and pushed into the bottom of the breast pocket to keep it open. The coin in the right hand is thumb palmed in the act of putting the coin into the left hand.

2. The right hand pulls up the left coat sleeve and the thumb palmed coin is brought near to the breast pocket.

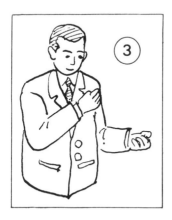
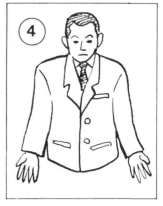

3. The left arm is extended as the sleeve is pulled up. Then the left arm is bent at the elbow and at the same time, the coin is dropped into the open breast pocket.

4. Both hands are opened to show the coin has vanished.

COIN PASSES THROUGH HANDKERCHIEF

EFFECT: A coin is dropped into glass and covered with a handkerchief. The coin passes through the handkerchief.

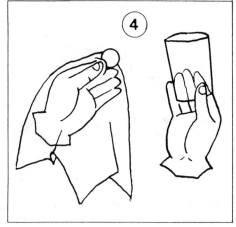

1. The picture shows the articles needed. They are a heavy man's pocket handkerchief which can not be seen through and a coin and a drinking glass.
2. The left hand is covered by the handkerchief.

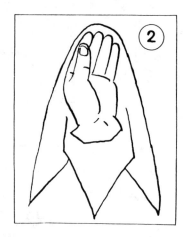

3. The coin is picked up with the right hand and trans-

ferred to the fingers of the left hand which is under the handkerchief. The coin is outside the handkerchief.

4. Pick up the glass with right hand and show it to the audience. The glass is held at the finger tips, some distance above the palm of the right hand.

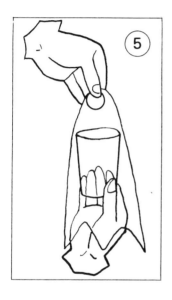

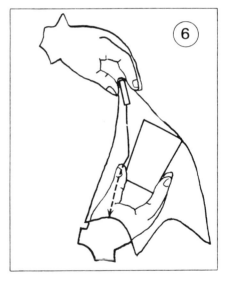

5. The left hand drapes the handkerchief over the top of the glass.

6. Under cover of the handkerchief, the glass is tipped a little towards the audience. The left hand drops the coin so that it hits against the side of the glass and this makes a sound like the coin had dropped into the glass.

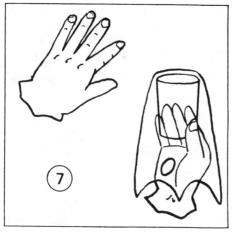
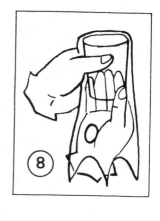

7. Coin is now in the palm of the right hand. The glass is straightened and the left hand releases the handkerchief so it falls over the glass.

8. The glass is now grasped thru the folds of the handkerchief.

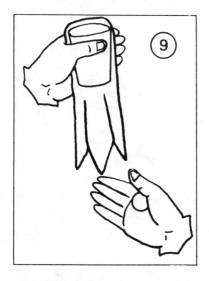
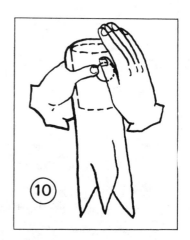

9. The right hand now thumb palms the coin and that hand is then brought out from under the handkerchief.

10. The right hand is now brought to the top of the edge of glass.

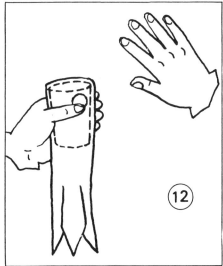

11. The left thumb is now put on top of the coin which had been thumb palmed and the right hand is brought down over the handkerchief and glass.

12. Now that the coin has been tranferred to the position where it is held by the left thumb, the right hand is raised and shown to be empty.

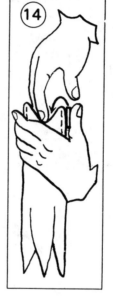

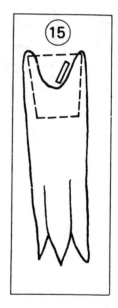

13. The right hand holds the four fingers together and makes a deep indentation in the handkerchief over the mouth of the glass.

14. The left thumb now pushed the coin up over the edge of the glass so that it falls into the indentation of the handkerchief. This action is hidden by the right fingers at this time.

15. The coin resting in the indentation of the handkerchief is shown in this picture.

16. The right hand holds the handkerchief at the bottom of the glass.

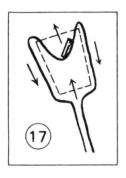

17. The left hand (not shown in this drawing) now slides the handkerchief down over the glass, removing the indentation.

18. The coin is caused to rise into view and the upper surface of the handkerchief is shown to the audience as the coin is allowed to drop to the table.

Han Ping Chien

Born in Tientsin, China, Han Ping Chien toured the United States in 1915 and 1916. When he appeared in Omaha he met David P. Abbott who exchanged many tricks with him and wrote a full page and a half review of his show for The Sphinx Magazine in August 1916.

Assisted by several young men and various members of his family, his show was well received throughout the country and the following method of passing a coin from one hand to another is but one of the many brilliant creations of this magical giant of the orient.

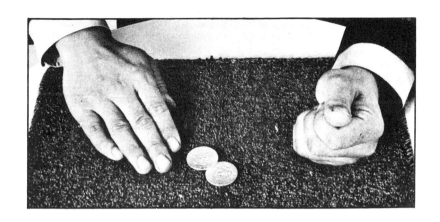

Chapter 7

Han Ping Chien Coin Move

In this move the coin held in the left hand is secretly passed into the right hand. This is a classic technique in Coin Magic and is adaptable for many coin tricks.

EXERCISE NO. 1. We will have a separate practice for each hand.

Part A Left hand.

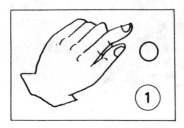

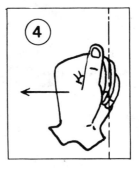

1. Put one coin on the table.
2. Pick up the coin with the left hand and close that hand into a fist. The left hand is resting on the table.

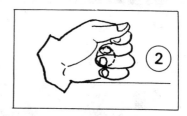

3. The fingers are relaxed slightly so that the coin drops to the surface of the table, resting on it's edge.
4. The left hand moves quickly about six inches to the left.

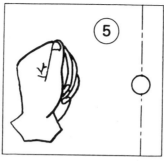

5. The coin stays at the same position on the table   The
   left hand is moved only and the fingers of the left hand
   do not move.

   This is important!

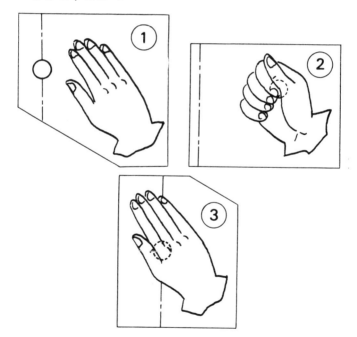

   Part B Right hand.
1. Lay the coin on the table.
2. Pick up the coin and put the coin into the thumb palm.
   The right hand moves about five inches to the right away

from where the coin had been resting on the table.

3. The right hand drops over the spot where the coin had been, with the fingers extended. Coin is still thumb palmed.

EXERCISE NO. 2. Han Ping Chien move using both hands.

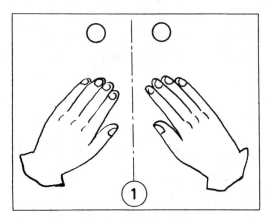

1. The two coins are placed on the table about seven inches apart. The dotted line in this picture represents the center of the table.

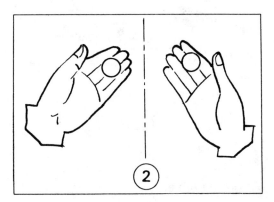

2. Both hands pick up a coin, one at a time, and the two coins are rested on top of the fingers as pictured. The

right hand coin is rested on the first two fingers in order to make the thumb palm easier to execute. The left hand has the coin over the two middle fingers.

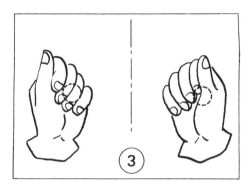

3. Both hands close over the coins in a fist. The right hand thumb palms the coin and the left hand is closed into a loose fist.

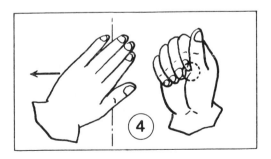

4. The left hand is slapped on to the center of the table so that the coin is heard as it hits the table.

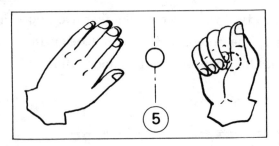

5. The left hand is then moved about six inches to the left so that the coin comes into view.

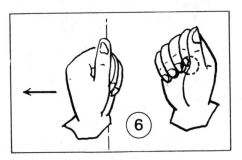

6. The left hand picks up the coin and that hand is rested on the table and the coin is allowed to slide down to the surface of the table where it is resting on it's edge with the left fingers loosely curled around the coin.

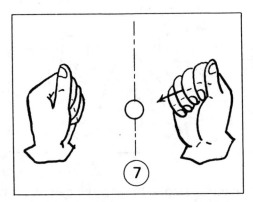

7. The coin is allowed to drop on to the table, at about

the center, as the left hand moves about six inches to the left.

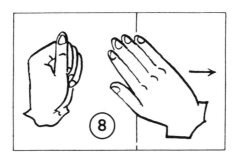

8. The right hand moves to cover over the coin which is resting on the table at the center. The coin in the right hand is now in the thumb palm position.

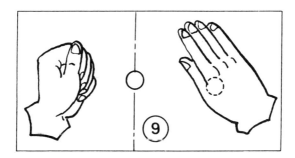

9. The right hand now moves back slowly about six inches to the right, so the audience can see the coin. The movement of the right hand and the left hand must be made at the same time. The coin on the table must look as though it dropped from the right hand the second time it comes into view.

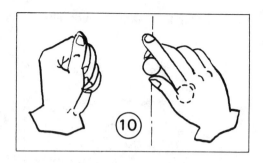

10. The right hand picks up the coin from the table and since a coin is thumb palmed in that hand at that time, it is difficult to use the forefinger, so it is suggested that you pick up the coin by using your middle finger and thumb.

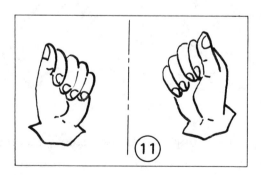

11. The audience must see that the closed fists are kept apart and they are moved slowly in the air for magical effect.

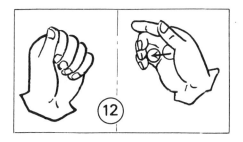

12. The thumb palmed coin is allowed to drop on the second coin held in that hand so the audience can hear the clicking sound.

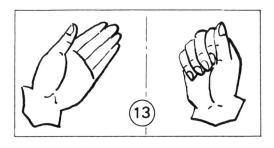

13. The left hand is opened to show the coin is gone.

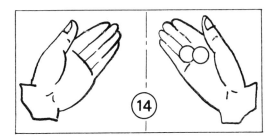

14. The right hand is slowly opened to show it has the two coins.

SEVERAL COINS PASS FROM ONE HAND TO ANOTHER

EFFECT: The performer is seated at the table. He has three silver coins in each hand and in addition there is one copper coin in the right hand. At the end of this trick, all of the coins are in the right hand.

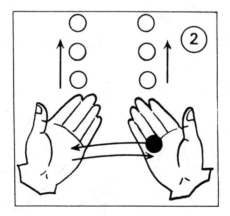

1. The six silver coins and the one copper coin are arranged on the table as shown in the drawing. The two hands are shown empty.

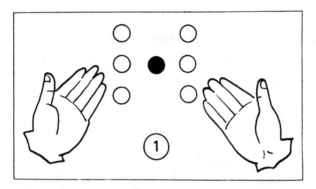

2. Pick up the copper coin with the right hand and then transfer it to the left hand and then return it to the right hand. The coin is moved from one hand to another a

few times and the two hands close quickly and the audience is asked to guess which hand is holding the coin The copper coin is actually in the right hand.

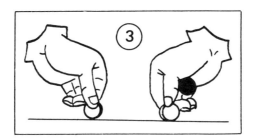

3. The copper coin is now finger palmed in the right hand and both the left hand and the right hand pick up the coins from the table, one by one so that there are finally three silver coins in each hand.

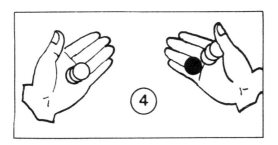

4. The left hand is now holding the three silver coins in an ordinary manner. This picture shows the left hand open, but when doing the trick, at this point, the left hand is closed. The right hand now holds all three silver coins in a thumb palm.

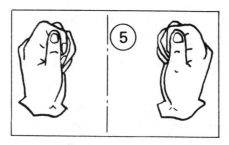

5. Both hands are closed into fists with the thumbs at the top and they are rested on the table about ten inches apart.

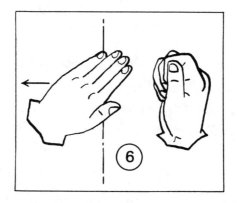

6. The left hand slaps down on the table.

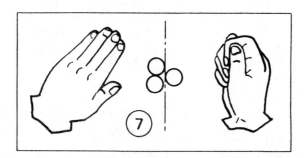

7. Right away, the left hand moves to the left about six inches so that the audience can see the three silver coins.

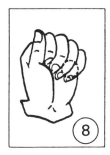
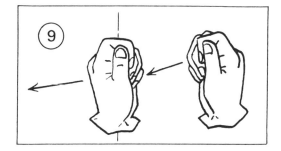

8. The three silver coins are now picked up and all three coins are allowed to slide down to the smallest finger.

9. The left hand is held loosely as a fist and it is rested on the table at about the same position as where the three coins had been resting.

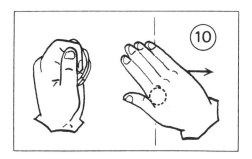

10. The left fist now moves about five inches to the left, at the same time, allowing the three coins from the left hand to fall on to the table. At the same time, the right fist is opened with all fingers outstretched, and with the three silver coins still thumb palmed, is put on the table to cover the three coins which had just been released from the left hand.

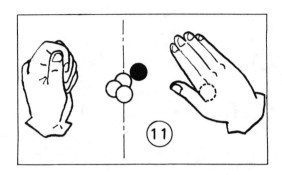

11. The copper coin is now released from the right hand at this time. After the copper coin is dropped, the right hand moves to the right so the audience can see the copper coin and the three silver coins on the center of the table. Thus it appears to the audience that the copper coin and the three silver coins all came from the right hand.

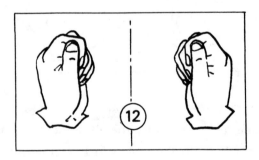

12. Pick up all the coins from the table, using the thumb and middle finger of the right hand. The three silver coins are still thumb palmed in that hand.

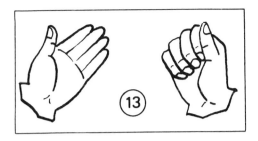

13. Performer now explains that he will pass the three coins from the left hand to the right hand. The left hand is opened to show it is empty.

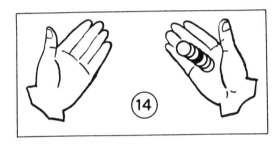

14. Open the right hand to show all the coins together.

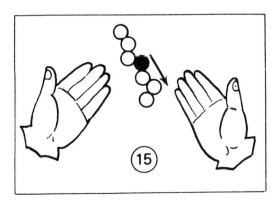

15. Drop all the coins, one at a time, on to the table.

COINS PASSING FROM HAND TO HAND

EFFECT: One copper coin and six silver coins are used. The right hand holds the copper coin and three silver coins. The left hand holds just three silver coins. The right hand goes under the table as the left hand hits the top of the table and that seems to cause all of the coins to assemble under the table. The left hand is found to be empty and the right hand brings out all the coins from under the table.

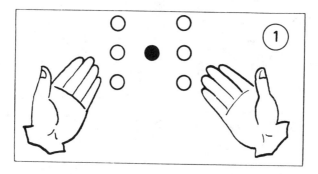

1. Arrange the coins on the table as pictured.

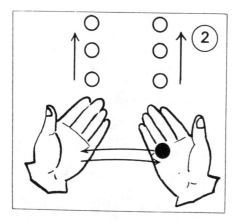

2. The right hand picks up the copper coin and places it into the right hand as the performer asks the audience if

they can be sure which hand is holding the copper coin. The coin having been transferred from hand to hand.

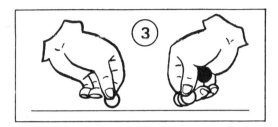

3. The right hand holds the copper coin in the finger palm position as both hands collect three coins and stack them on the table and then each hand picks up the stack of three silver coins.

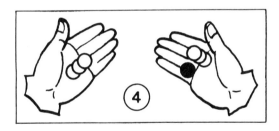

4. Each hand is opened to show the three silver coins and the right hand is shown in this picture holding the copper coin separate from the others.

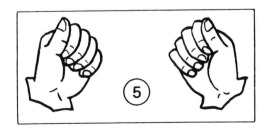

5. Both hands are closed into fists.

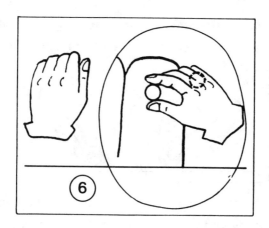

6. The right hand goes under the table and the left fist is held about ten inches above the top of the table. The right fist hits the underside of the table. Then the right hand deposits the stack of three silver coins on top of the right leg, above the knee.

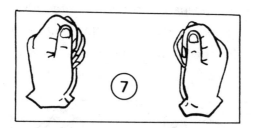

7. The performer seems to have changed his mind and after having hit the underside of the table once or twice, he says, "You may not believe that the coins are still in this hand."

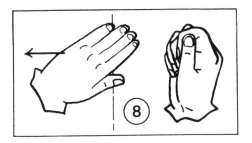

8. The left hand then slaps the three silver coins on to the top of the table.

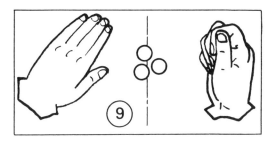

9. The left hand is then moved a few inches to the left as the performer says, "You see, we still have the three coins in this hand."

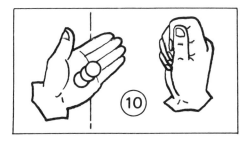

10. The three coins are again placed on the left palm which is opened to show the audience that the coins are together.

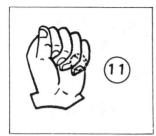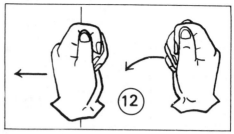

11. The left hand is closed into a fist and the fist is rested on top of the table with the thumb uppermost and the three coins are allowed to slide down to the position where they are held in the fist by just the smallest finger.

12. Having deposited the stack of silver coins on the right knee, the right hand, closed into a fist, is brought back from under the table and here we see the two fists on the table. The left fist is resting on the imaginary center line of the table top.

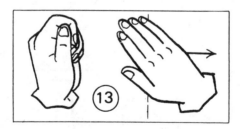

13. The left hand is brought away about six inches from the center of the table. As the left hand moves, the little finger opens alightly allowing the three silver coins to drop on to the table. The right hand is opened at this time and is brought face down on top of the three silver coins, dropping the copper coin at that time.

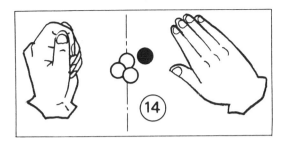

14. The right hand is then moved away to show the audience the copper coin resting with the three silver coins. "Here are the other coins," the performer says, as the right hand is drawn away.

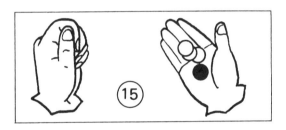

15. These four coins are now picked up by the right hand and are shown on the open right palm.

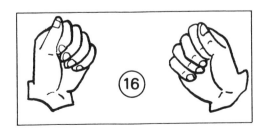

16. The right hand is closed into a fist.

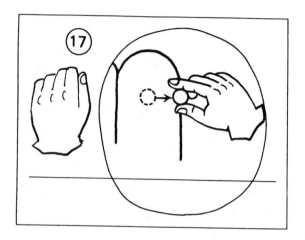

17. The right fist goes under the table, and this time the right hand picks up the three silver coins which had been resting on the right leg. At the same time, the left fist is held about ten inches above the top of the table.

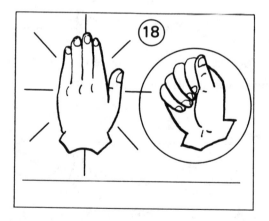

18. The left hand is slapped down on the table top with the palm open and at the same time, the right hand, under the table, shakes the coins in that hand.

19. The left hand is turned over to show it is empty.

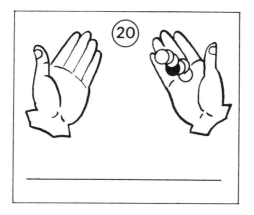

20. The right hand is brought out from under the table and the audience sees all the coins in that hand.

The coins are now dropped on the table, one coin at a time. Here we have two versions of COINS PASSING FROM HAND TO HAND and it is often wise to present the two together as a "routine." This repetition of an effect, using two different methods will confuse the audience.

Dai Vernon

Born on June 11, 1894 in Ottawa, Canada, Dai Vernon started performing magic tricks as a small boy and has continued to excell in this art form to the extent that he is known as a "legend in his own time".

Dai Vernon Performed professionaly for many years until 1955 when he began traveling to England and to many cities in the United States with his lecture. He came to Hollywood in 1965 to visit his friend, Jay Ose at The Magic Castle and has remained there to this day as it's most respected resident.

Dai Vernon has written several books giving his own "inner secrets" as well as books on the magic of Nat Leipzig and Max Malini. "SELECT SECRETS" and "EARLY VERNON" are two excellent books for the beginner.

Chapter 8

The Classic Palm

This technique of coin magic uses both the fingers and the palm of the hand. When you have learned to use this palm, the five fingers can be used while the coin is secretly held in the palm of the hand. This sleight should be mastered by the magician as it has great value and is part of so many coin tricks.

EXERCISE NO. 1. Holding the coin.

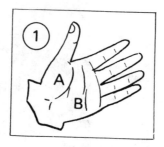

1. Hold your left palm open and pinch the area marked A and B in this picture. Your right fingers should be able to grasp the flesh at points A and B.

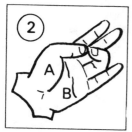 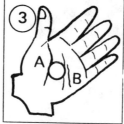 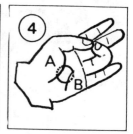

2. Touch your left thumb to the tip of the third finger and then the flesh at point A and point B is more pronounced.

3. Open your left palm and put a coin into the space between point A and B. Use a large coin for this exercise.

4. Once again bring your thumb to the tip of the third finger as the coin is held by the flesh at point A and B. You will find that the coin is held securely and will not drop, even when the hand is turned over.

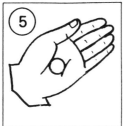 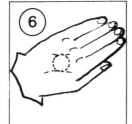 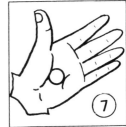

5. The thumb is brought away from the third finger and brought next to the first finger in a natural manner as the coin is still grasped by the flesh at point A and B.

6. The hand is turned over and held in a natural position while the coin is hidden in the palm.

7. Do not worry about the shape or appearance of the hand. Think only that the coin is held securely. Do not allow the thumb to be extended as shown.

 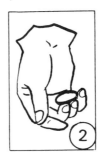 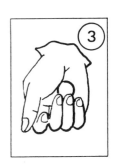

EXERCISE NO. 2. Using only one hand.

1. The left hand has its fingers extended down towards the floor. The coin is rested on the extreme tips of the two middle fingers.

2. The two middle fingers curl up and bring the coin into the center of the left palm as the palm is spread open.

3. Press the coin deep into the palm as the flesh catches the edge of the coin.

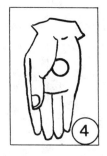 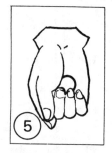

4. The two middle fingers are removed from the coin and are allowed to extend in a natural position.

5. When the two fingers put the coin into the palm, try to hold your thumb next to the forefinger.

EXERCISE NO. 3.   Producing the coin from the palm position.

Part A

1. Using the right hand, the coin is held in the classic palm.

2. Bend the middle finger, bringing the finger tip to the lower edge of the coin, so that the coin is pushed away from palm.

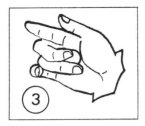
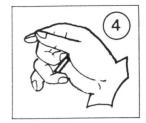

3. Bend the ring finger so that the tip of that finger catches the upper edge of the coin.

4. Pull ring finger so that the coin comes forward, away from the palm, pivoting on it's lower edge.

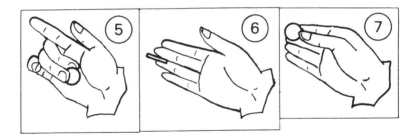

5. Continue to pull ring finger and thus the middle and ring fingers are able to pinch the coin.

6. Extend the two fingers with the coin clipped between them.

7. Thumb pushes from the underside of the coin to bring it into the position where it is pressed against the tip of the forefinger by the thumb.

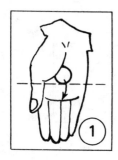 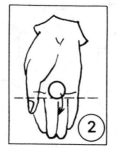 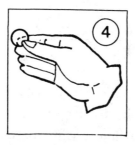

Part B

1. Coin is classic palmed with the fingers pointing down.
2. Release the pressure of the base of the the thumb on the coin, so that it flips over on to the lower part of the palm.
3. Coin flips once more in the direction of the forefinger.

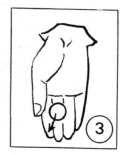

4. Put thumb on coin and push the coin up between the tips of the forefinger and thumb so that it can be better seen by the audience.

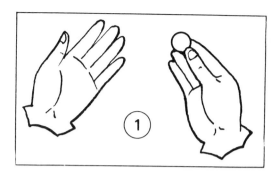

EXERCISE NO. 4. Making the coin vanish.

Part A

1. Show the coin in right hand. Hold the left palm upward.

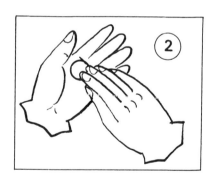 

2. Coin is brought to the left palm by the right fingers which are still holding the coin.

3. Coin is brought to the classic palm in the right hand.

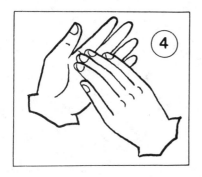 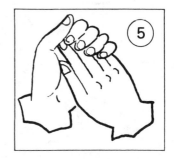

4. The right hand seems to be in the same position as in #2 when the coin was first brought to the left palm.

5. Left fingers are closed around the extended fingers of the right hand. This action begins as soon as the coin touches the left palm. The left fingers conceal the movement of the right hand as it brings the coin to the classic palm position.

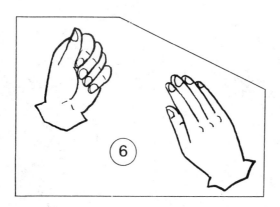

6. The closed left hand is brought away from the right hand. The movement is to the left and a bit forward. The performer directs his attention to his left fist.
   Open left hand to show the coin has vanished.

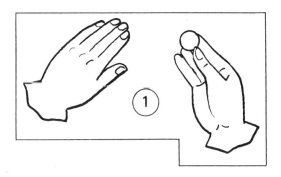

Part B

1. Coin is held at the finger tip of right forefinger. The coin is held at the performer's chest height for emphasis and to attract the audience's attention. The left palm is turned downward.

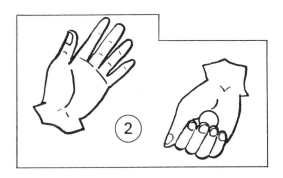

2. Left hand is brought forward and turned over to show the palm empty. The right hand comes closer to the performer's chest as the left hand is extended and attracts the audience's attention. The coin is classic palmed in the right hand.

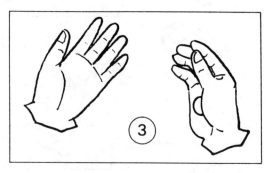

3. The performer pretends to hold a coin at the tips of his raised right hand. At that moment, the performer directs his gaze into the spectator's eyes.

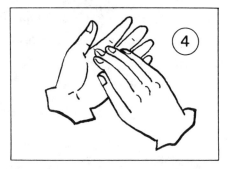

4. The performer then acts like he is putting the coin from the right finger tips into the left palm. At this point, the right fingers are all held tightly together.

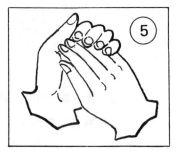

5. When right hand comes to the left palm, the left fingers curl around the fingers of the right hand.

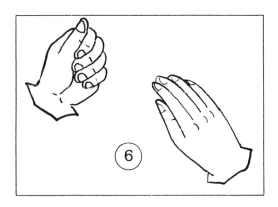

6. Left hand is now closed into a fist and brought away from the right hand, as it moves to the left and a bit forward. Performer keeps watching his left fist.

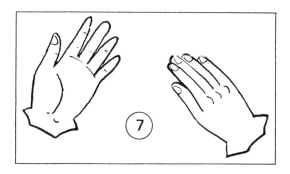

7. The left hand is opened to show the coin has vanished.

THE CLICK PASS

This technique of coin magic is used often as part of a longer routine. It appears to the audience that two coins are picked up with the left hand. As the second coin is picked up, the audience can hear the sound of the first coin being hit by the second coin. However, when the two hands are opened, there is one coin in each hand.

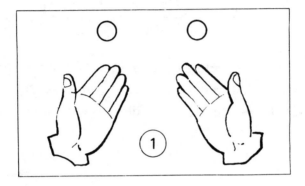

1. Two coins are resting on the table and the two palms are shown empty.

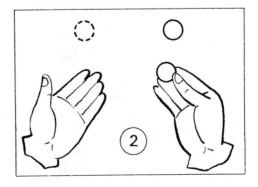

2. The right hand picks up the coin which was in front of the left hand.

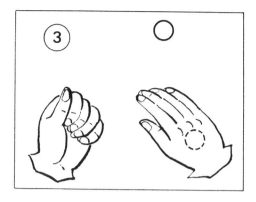

3. The right hand acts as though it places this coin into the left hand. Actually, the coin remains in the right hand in an ordinary palm position.

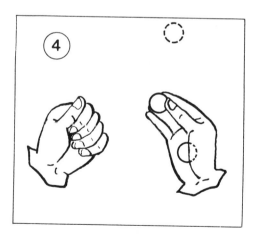

4. The right hand picks up the right coin, using the thumb and middle and ring fingers.

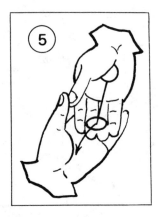 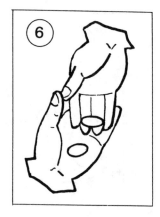

5. The left fist is opened slightly and the right finger tips go into the left palm. The coin which is palmed in the right hand is now allowed to drop down so that it hits the coin which is held by the right finger tips. That coin makes a clicking sound as it hits the second coin and continues on into the left palm.

6. The left hand now has the dropped coin.

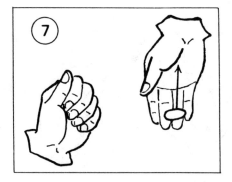

7. The right hand is removed from the left hand palm as the left hand closes into a fist and the right hand then brings the coin from the finger tips to the classic palm position.

124

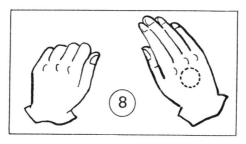

8. The right hand fingers are extended slightly so that the hand looks empty.

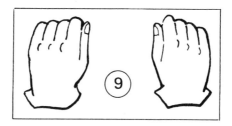

9. The left hand is now closed into a fist. The left fist makes a gesture of invisably passing something over to the right.

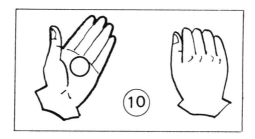

10. The left hand is opened and only one coin is seen.
    The right hand is then opened to reveal the missing coin.

This same maneuver can be used to give the effect of a coin passing from one hand to another hand which is under the table.

COINS ACROSS (Version No. 3)

EFFECT: The performer crosses his arms and holds one coin in each hand. The arms are un-crossed and the hands are opened to show both coins are now in one hand.

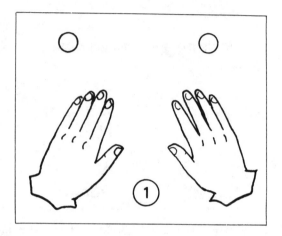

1. The two coins are resting on the table about eight inches apart.

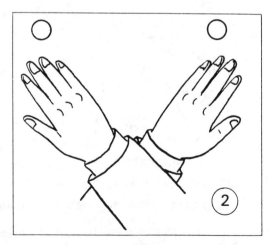

2. The two arms now cross, with the right hand going over the left hand. The arms cross above the wrists.

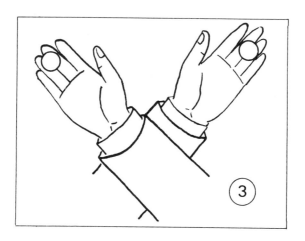

3. Each hand picks up one coin and each coin rests on top of the finger tips. The right hand must get ready to put the coin into the classic palm position.

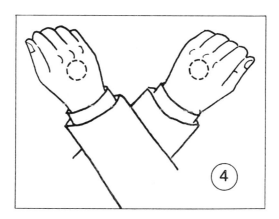

4. Both hands are closed into fists and the two fists are turned over so that the backs are uppermost.

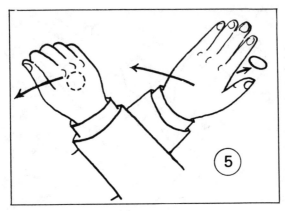

5. In a gesture to show the audience that one coin is in
each hand, the performer moves both his hands up from
the table and away from the table slightly to the left.
This movement is shown by the two arrows. At the
same time, the left hand in opened, dropping the coin on
the table.

6. The left hand picks up the coin from the table and this
time the coin is held in the fist by just the smallest
finger. The thumb in the fist pushes the coin down to
the little finger. The fist is held with the back uppermost, but in this picture the fist is turned so that the
reader can see the position of the coin under the little
finger.

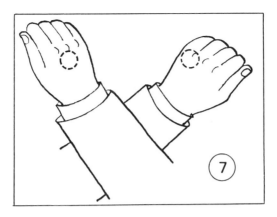

7. Both fists are closed as before.

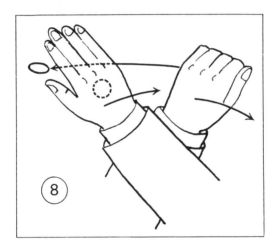

8. This time the two hands are brought up from the table and swing slightly to the right as shown by the two arrows in the picture. The coin held by the left little finger is now released and dropped on to the table as the right fist is opened and the extended right fingers give the impression that this coin came from the right hand. The right hand still has a coin in the classic palm position.

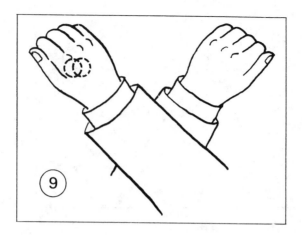

9. The right hand now picks up the coin from the table and carefully adds it to the one which is palmed in that hand and that hand is closed into a fist.

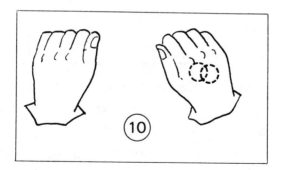

10. Very slowly the two hands are separated so that the right hand is brought over to the right side of the table and the two fists are held some distance apart.

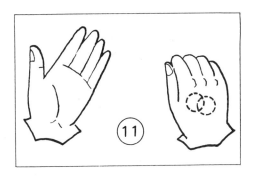

11. The two fists are rotated slowly as the performer explains that he will cause the coin to pass from the left hand to the right. The left hand is then shown empty.

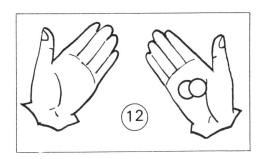

12. The right hand is opened to show the two coins.

Here are two added notes. When the coin is dropped from the left hand, (see Drawing No. 8) the right hand must be held open in a relaxed position to give the impression that the right is then empty and the coin on the table came from that hand.

This version of COINS ACROSS can be performed with the coin going into the thumb palm instead of the classic palm as described in Drawing No. 4. Either technique can be used in this effect.

John Scarne

Born around the turn of the century in Steubenville, Ohio. John Scarne is one of the best known authorities on games and gambling. His lectures for the military brought him great aclaim around the world.

John Scarne is also one of the best known magicians in the world since his books have had such a wide circulation and also he has made a most successful movie on gambling and his many performances on the television and lecture platforms have been viewed by millions.

He is best recognized as the author of "SCARNE ON CARDS" and "SCARNE ON DICE" and yet his book, "SCARNE ON MAGIC TRICKS" contains 200 excellent tricks, done with common objects, and without any sleight of hand.

132

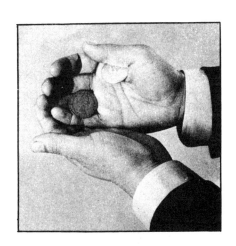

Chapter 9

The Coin Change

This technique in Coin Magic is often used to change a copper coin into a silver coin. There are many effects which use this method of changing one coin into another.

EXERCISE NO. 1. Using the right hand.

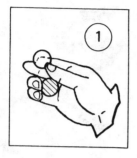 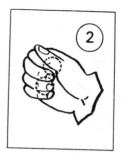

1. The copper coin is finger palmed. The silver coin is held at the finger tips of the right hand.
2. As the right fist closes, the first finger and middle finger push the silver coin back to the base of the thumb and that coin is then thumb palmed.

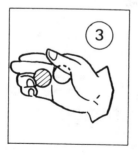 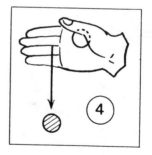

3. This shows the silver coin thumb palmed while the copper coin is finger palmed.
4. The copper coin is dropped on the table as the fingers are extended and the silver coin remains in the thumb palm.

EXERCISE NO. 2. Using two hands.

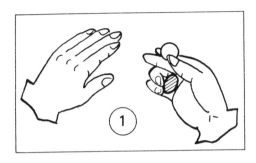

1. The copper coin is finger palmed and the silver coin is
   held at the right finger tips. The left hand is held with
   the palm down.

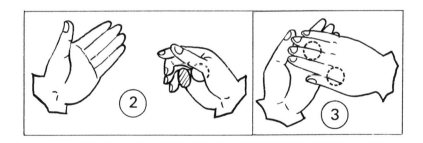

2. The left palm is shown empty and at the same time, the
   silver coin is thumb palmed in right hand.
3. The copper coin is now dropped into the left palm.

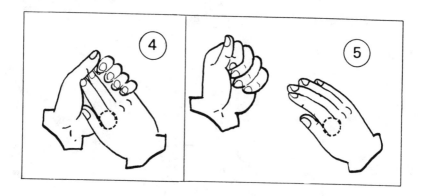

4. The left fingers close around the coin as the right hand is removed.

5. The right hand is lowered slightly as the left hand is raised a bit. This is to cause the audience to look at that hand.

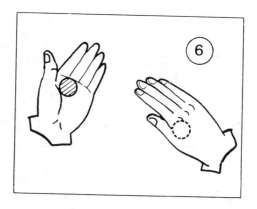

6. The left hand is opened to show the copper coin.

John Scarne's COPPER TO SILVER

EFFECT: The spectator is given a copper coin to hold while the performer holds a silver coin. When the magician counts to three, the spectator finds that he is holding the silver coin and the performer is holding the copper coin.

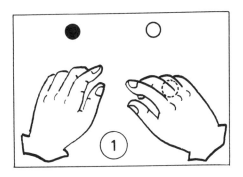

1. Two silver coins are in the performer's right side pocket and one copper coin is in his left side pocket. Before starting to perform this trick, the performer places both hands into his pockets and with his right hand he puts one silver coin into the finger palm and holds the other silver coin at the finger tips. The left hand holds the copper coin at the finger tips. These coins are withdrawn and one silver coin and one copper coin are placed on the table.

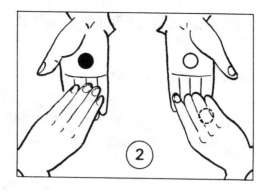

2. The spectator is asked to extend his two hands. A copper coin is placed in his right palm and a silver coin is placed in his left palm.

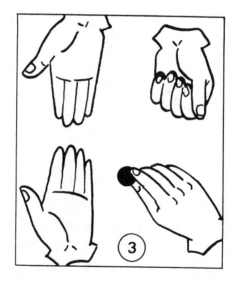

3. The spectator is asked to close his left hand over the silver coin. The performer picks up the copper coin from the open right hand.

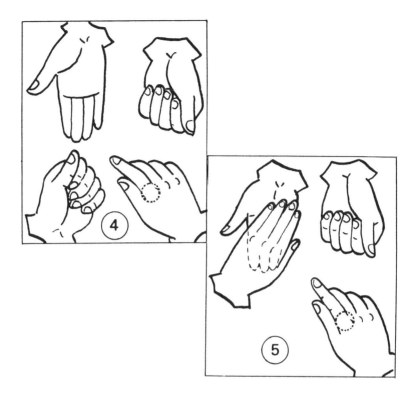

4. Thumb palm the copper coin in your right hand as you pretend putting that coin into the left hand. Actually, the finger palmed silver coin is dropped into the performer's left hand as that hand closes over the coin. This is done so that no one can see that the coin is silver and not copper.

5. The performer now requests the spectator to close his hand as quickly as possible over the second coin. The silver coin from the performer's left hand is carefully dropped on the spectator's open right and which is then quckly closed into a fist. This fist is then turned over so the back is uppermost.

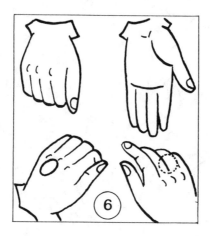

6. The copper coin in the right hand is now changed to the finger palm from the thumb palm and the spectator is asked to open his left hand. The performer grasps the silver coin by his right thumb and forefinger and it is placed on the back of his left fist.

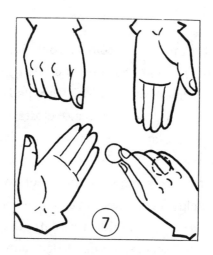

7. The right hand again picks up the silver coin as the left hand is now turned palm up.

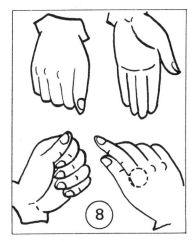

8. The silver coin is now thumb palmed in the right hand as the copper coin is dropped from the finger palm into the left hand.

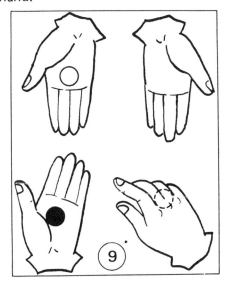

9. The performer says, "One, two, three", and then the spectator is asked to open his right hand. He finds that he is holding the silver coin and then the performeer shows that he has the copper coin in his left hand.

T. Nelson Downs

Born on March 26, 1867 in Montour, Iowa. Thomas N. Downs aquired his manipulative skill while working as a railroad ticket agent and telegrapher. By that time he was reportedly "receiving one of the largest salaries of any variety hall performer in New York City."

In 1899 he was booked for a two weeks engagement at The Palace Theatre in London and he remained for six months. He went on to tour the largest theatres in all the important cities of Europe.

T. Nelson Downs is best remembered for his version of "The Miser's Dream", an effect where he produced a great many silver coins at his fingertips.

One of the finest books for the coin magician was written by John N. Hilliard and T. Nelson Downs under the title," THE ART OF MAGIC."

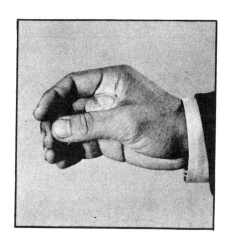

Chapter 10

The T. Nelson Downs Palm

This move is credited to the great Coin Magician, T. Nelson Downs and it is often used in coin effects suitable for the stage. For this palm, coins the size of an American half dollar should be used.

EXERCISE NO. 1 Holding the coin.

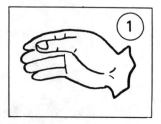

1. The right thumb, first finger and middle finger are used. The hand is held as in the drawing and the thumb is held so that it covers the space between the first and second finger. The thumb is extended as far as possible.

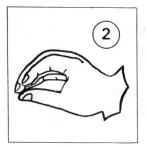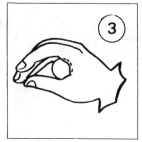

2. This view from the top shows the space between the thumb and first finger.

3. The coin must be held tightly in this space between the thumb and first finger.

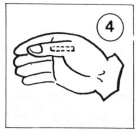

4. This shows how the hand holding the coin in the Down's palm is seen by the audience.

EXERCISE NO. 2 Learning to put the coin into Down's Palm, using one hand.

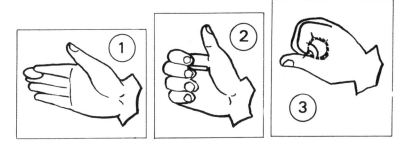

1. Hold the coin between the first and second fingers.
2. Excepting for the thumb, all the fingers curl inward. The coin will hit the base of the thumb. The drawing shows the thumb up in the air for clarity of the explanation. Actually, the thumb is extended towards the finger tips.
3. Top view, showing the coin in the position of the Down's Palm.

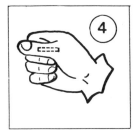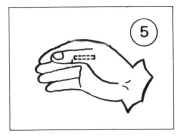

4. Front view of the hand as it is seen by the audience.
5. After the coin is tightly grasped by the thumb, the four fingers are relaxed and are extended.

EXERCISE NO. 3 Producing the coin from Down's Palm.

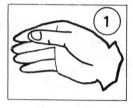  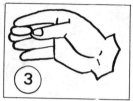

1. The coin is held by Down's palm and the palm of the hand is held facing the audience.
2. The thumb is out-stretched and all the four fingers now curl in towards the base of the thumb and the coin is clipped between the first and second fingers.
3. The thumb relaxes it's grip on the coin and the first and second fingers uncurl to bring the coin forward.

4. The thumb is put under the coin and flips it to an upright position.

EXERCISE NO. 4. Production of several coins.

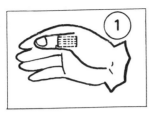 

1. Four half dollars are held in the Down's palm position.

2. The second and third fingers curl in and the top of the second finger comes under the bottom coin.

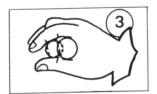 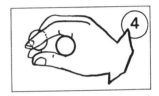

3. The second finger presses against the bottom coin slightly and that coin is released so that it rests on the top of the second finger.

4. The second finger is now outstretched with the coin resting on it. Care must be taken that the other coins are not disturbed.

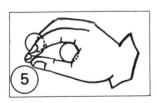 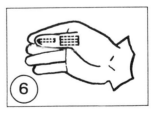

5. After the second finger is outstretched, clip the coin between the first and second fingers. The thumb now pushes the coin towards the back of the hand.

6. Drawing shows the front of the hand. Up to this point, the audience has not seen the coin.

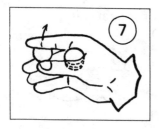 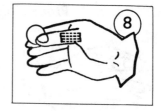

7. Using the thumb, the coin is pressed against the second finger and at the same time, the first finger is withdrawn from the coin.

8. After the first finger has been withdrawn, it is brought back behind the coin and it pushes the coin into an upright position so that the thumb and first finger is then holding the coin.

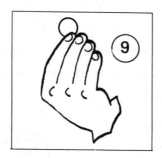

9. At this point, the entire hand can be turned so that the audience can see the back of the hand. The coin can be dropped or placed into the left hand. This move is then repeated for the other three coins. When producing the last coin, you do the moves described in Exercise No. 3 and bend all four fingers since you will then be producing a single coin from the Down's palm.

HANDKERCHIEF AND COIN. (Version No. 2)

EFFECT: Handkerchief is shown empty and draped over the left hand. A coin placed in the handkerchief is vanished and then reproduced.

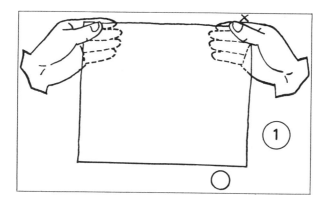

1. Performer has coin on the table and he shows the pocket handkerchief by holding it at two corners as shown in the drawing. This should be a heavy cloth handkerchief.

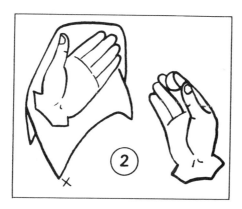

2. This handkerchief is now draped over the empty left hand. The coin is picked up with the right hand and is held ready to be placed into the Down's palm position.

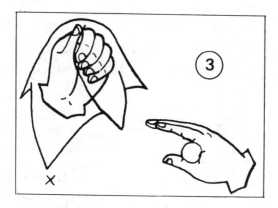

3. The right hand acts as though the coin is placed inside the handkerchief which is in the left hand. Actually the coin is put into the Down's palm in the right hand. This drawing shows a "top view" of the two hands.

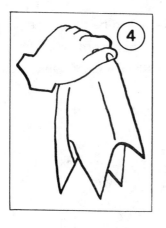

4. The left hand turns over and allows the four corners of the handkerchief to hang and the performer acts like he is holding the coin inside the handkerchief.

5. Another view of the left hand and handkerchief.

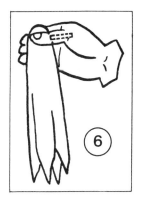 

6. The handkerchief is now transferred to the right hand so that it is now held by the thumb and first finger.

7. One corner of the handkerchief is lifted by the left hand and it is clipped by the first and second fingers of the right hand.

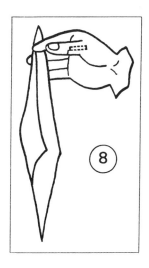

8. The back of the right hand is turned towards the audience and the thumb is relaxed from the center of the

handkerchief. The handkerchief is now hanging from just one corner and it appears to the audience that the coin has been caused to vanish.

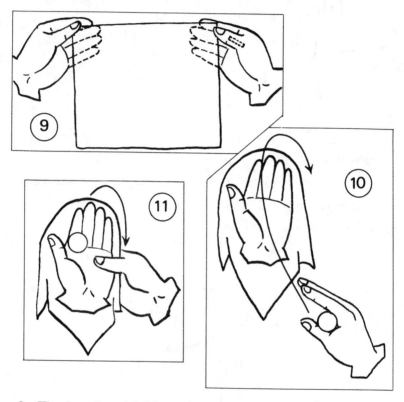

9. The handkerchief is again outstretched between the two hands as it is shown to the audience.
10. The handkerchief is again draped over the left hand with the fingers pointing upwards. The back of the hand is towards the audience. This shows the performer's view.
11. This is also the performer's view. The coin is now dropped into the center of the handkerchief as the performer makes a few magical passes over the handkerchief.

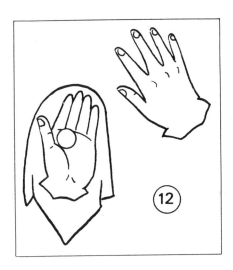

·12. The right hand is now held so that the audience can see it is empty.

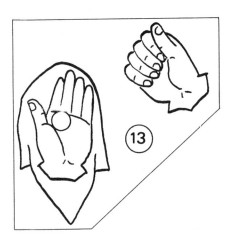

13. The performer now gestures as though he is catching a coin from the air as he closes his right hand into a fist.

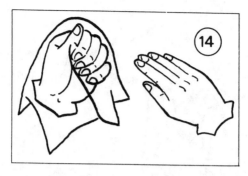

14. The performer now acts as though he is throwing the imaginary coin into the left hand which is covered by the handkerchief. The left hand is then closed into a fist.

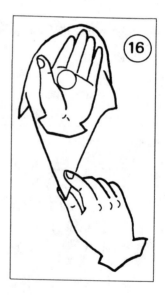

15. The performer now grasps a corner of the handkerchief which is nearest to his body.

16. The left hand is now opened and lowered so that the audience can see into the center of the handkerchief and the coin is revealed.

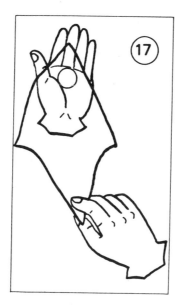

17. The right hand continues to pull the corner of the hand-
    kerchief slowly so that the coin slides from the center of
    the handkerchief into the palm of the left hand.

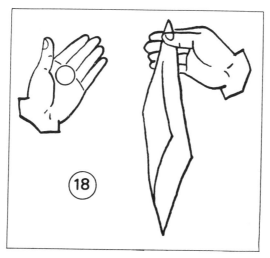

18. The handkerchief and coin are shown at the end of the
    effect.

PRODUCTION OF FOUR COINS FROM THE AIR

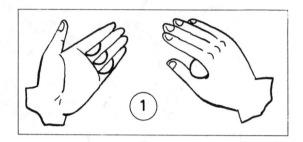

1. PREPARATION: Four coins are needed. Three coins
   are held in the left hand, clipped between the four
   fingers as shown in the drawing. The coins are clipped
   well back near the base of the fingers. It is important
   that the coins can not be seen from the back of the left
   hand. One coin is held in the Down's palm in the right
   hand.

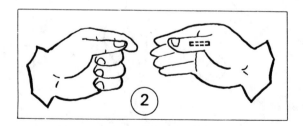

2. The left hand is closed into a lightly held fist around the
   three hidden coins.

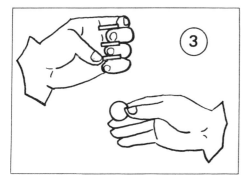 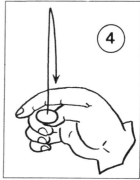

3. The right hand produces one coin from the Down's palm. At the same time, the left thumb prepares to push out the coin which is held between the small finger and the third finger.

4. The right hand flips the produced coin up in the air and catches it. This action shows the audience there is nothing else in that hand.

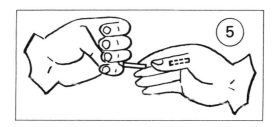

5. The right hand now acts as though the flipped coin is being placed between the small finger and the third finger. However, that coin is actually replaced into the Down's palm in the right hand as the left thumb pushes out the coin which had been hidden between the two smallest fingers of the left hand.

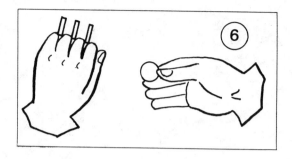

6. The same move is repeated with the next three coins. Each time a coin is produced from the Down's palm, it is flipped in the air and then the performer appears to be placing that coin between the fingers of the left hand.

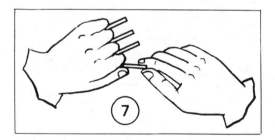

7. When the fourth and last coin is produced, the left hand is turned so that the thumb is now nearest to the floor and the coin is placed between the thumb and the top of the forefinger.

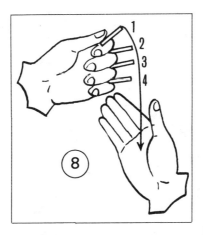

8. The left fist is turned again, once all four coins are held and then the left thumb is uppermost. The coin between the thumb and forefinger is dropped first as the performer counts, "One".

The coin below that one is dropped into the performer's right hand as he counts, "Two". This is continued until all four coins have been dropped and counted into the right hand.

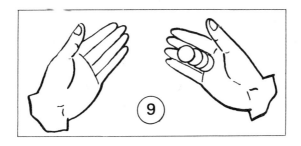

9. The right hand is now holding the four coins which had been produced from thin air.

Slydini

Tony Slydini was born in Foggia, Italy in 1900. He lived in Buenos Aires, Argentina until 1930 when he came to the United States. He performed in Dime Museums and illusion shows throughout the country until he moved to Boston in 1940.

Slydini has been a teacher of magic in New York City since 1947. Since then he has appeared on several television programs and occasionally in night clubs, but primarily he lectures at the leading magic conventions and has toured the magic clubs of the United States, England and Europe.

Slydini has written several fine books with a great many photographic illustrations. "SLYDINI ENCORES" has 157 pages and hundreds of illustrations with many different effects including several coin routines.

Chapter 11

The French Drop

This is a basic technique in Coin Magic and is very often used to vanish or exchange a coin.

EXERCISE NO. 1. Using just the left hand.

  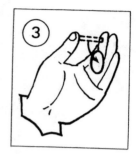

1. The left hand holds the coin with the thumb and tip of middle finger. The four fingers are held tightly together. This is the view the performer has looking at the hand from above.
2. This is the side view of the same position.
3. Remove the thumb from the coin so that the coin will drop down to the base of the middle finger.

4. The coin is then finger palmed. The left hand is turned over so the palm is facing the floor.

EXERCISE NO. 2. Using both hands.

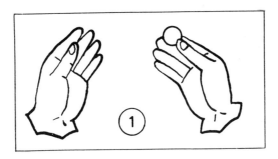

1. The right hand holds the coin at the finger tips and it is shown to the audience.

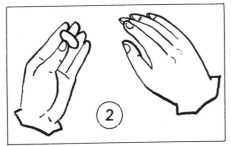
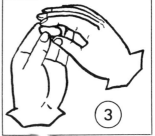

2. The coin is now handed or to the left hand where it is held by the thumb and middle finger.
3. The right hand acts as though it is grabbing the coin. The right thumb goes under the coin and the left thumb at that time is removed from the edge of the coin and this allows the coin to drop down to the base of the middle finger.

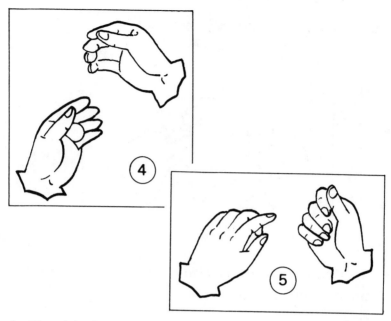

4. The right hand now acts like it is closing about the coin and at the same time, the left hand has the coin finger palmed. At this time, the right hand is raised slightly and this helps to attract the audience's attention.

5. The right hand is now closed into a fist as the left hand is turned over and then slowly is lowered to the performer's side.

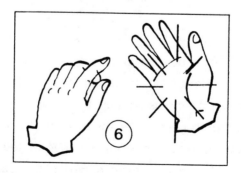

6. The right hand is opened to show the coin has vanished.

SILVER AND COPPER

EFFECT: The silver and copper coins are wapped in a handkerchief. The spectator selects either the silver or copper and it is seen that the chosen coin has vanished from the handkerchief.

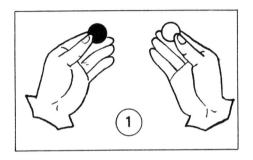

1. The right hand holds the silver coin and the left hand holds the copper coin.

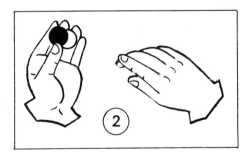

2. The two coins are now held in position for performing the french drop. The coins are separated slightly as shown in the drawing.

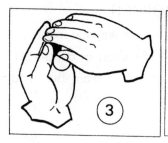
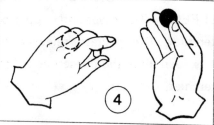

3. The right hand appears to grab the two coins. Actually, the bottom (silver) coin is dropped into the left hand.

4. The right hand is now holding just the copper coin but the audience thinks it is holding both coins. The left hand is now holding the silver coin in the finger palm position.

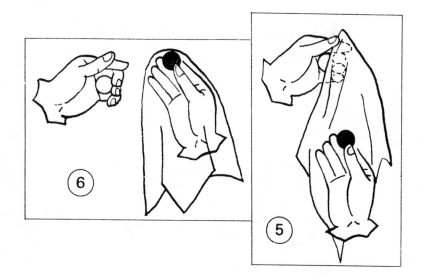

5. The left hand picks up the handkerchief by one corner so that it hangs loosely.

6. The handkerchief is now draped over the right hand which is holding the copper coin.

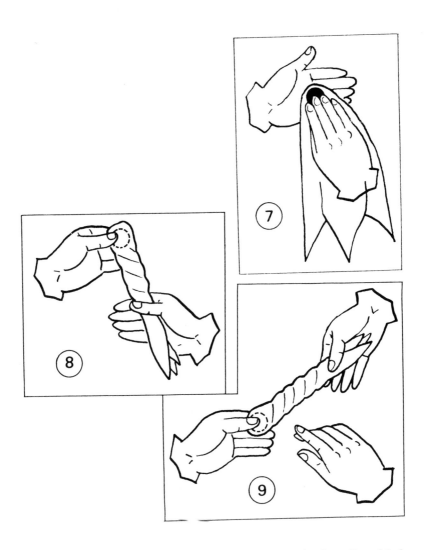

7. The copper coin has been covered by the handkerchief and this covered coin is now placed directly over the silver coin which is resting in the palm of the left hand.

8. The two coins are now held together as the handkerchief is twisted several times.

9. The spectator is asked to hold the four corners of the twisted handkerchief.

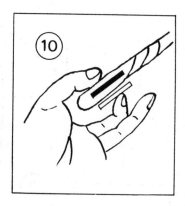

10. This drawing shows that the copper coin is within the folds of the handkerchief and the silver coin is held even with the other coin, but it is actually under the handkerchief.

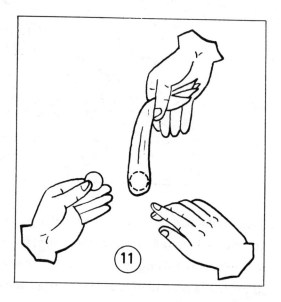

11. The spectator is asked to pull the handkerchief and then it is seen that the silver coin is now free from the handkerchief and in the left hand.

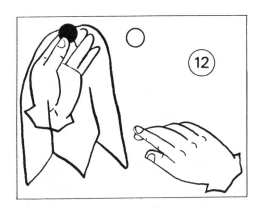

12. The silver coin is placed on the table and the copper coin is grasped by the left hand, thru the cloth, and the handkerchief is then unfolded so the audience can see that the copper coin is indeed inside the handkerchief.

The copper coin is placed on the table alongside the silver coin and the handkerchief is also placed on the table as the performer shows both his hands to be empty.

It should be explained that in the first part of this trick, the spectator is asked to indicate his preference. The performer asks, "Do you want the silver coin or the copper coin?"

If the spectator says, "Silver", the performer replies, "Very well. I will remove the silver coin and the copper coin will be left in the handkerchief." On the other hand, if the spectator answers, "Copper", the performer says, "Very well, I will remove the silver coin and the COPPER coin will be left in the handkerchief. This is known as giving the spectator the "magician's choice".

Tenkai

Born on December 1, 1889 in Nagoya, Japan, Tenkai Ishida became interested in the art of magic around the age of eight. Eventually he became a member of the Tenkatsu troupe of magicians that traveled to the United States.

During the golden era of vaudeville, Tenkai and Okinu toured the circuits of Pantages, Keith-Albee, R.K.O. and Orpheum. He had several appearances on Broadway in New York City at the famed Hippodrome and Palace Theatres.

Tenkai was recognized by his fellow magicians around the world as being one of the greatest sleight of hand artists and was well loved by his associates.

"THE MAGIC OF TENKAI" by Gerald Kosky and Arnold Furst was published by Magic Limited in 1974 and this large volume contains many coin tricks as well as other effects created by one of Japan's greatest magicians.

Chapter 12

Coin And Playing Card

HOW TO HIDE COIN BEHIND PLAYING CARD

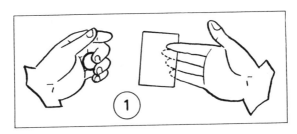

1. The coin is finger palmed in left hand and the card is held in the right hand, between the first and second fingers. This is the performer's view of the two hands.

 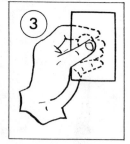 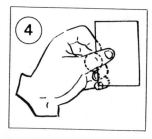

2. The card is now held in the left hand with the coin hidden under the card.

3. Under cover of the card, the coin is pushed from the finger palm position to where it is held by the tips of the middle and ring fingers.

4. The thumb remains in position, but the middle and ring fingers curl a little bit so that the coin goes almost into the palm of the left hand.

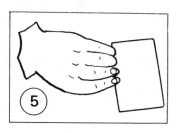 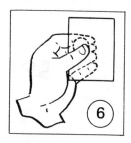

5. The left hand is now turned over with the palm down so that the back of the left hand can be seen and also the back of the card is in view.

6. The left hand is turned again so that the thumb is up and the fingers are outstretched behind the card. The face of the card is seen while the coin remains hidden.

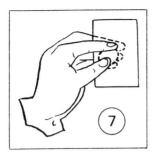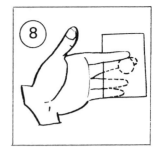

7. The left forefinger is now brought to the face of the card and the coin is clipped by the first finger and middle finger as it remains hidden behind the card.

8. The thumb is removed so that it appears that the card is held by the two fingers only.

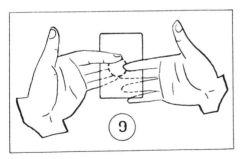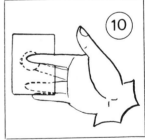

9. The right hand now extends the right forefinger and that finger goes on top of the face of the card. The middle finger goes under the card to grasp the coin behind the card.

10. The left hand is now removed and the right hand now appears to be holding just the playing card.

COINS PRODUCED FROM PLAYING CARDS

EFFECT: Two playing cards are shown and when separated slightly, a coin is produced. The two cards are shown again and then a secons coin is produced.

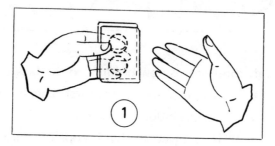

1. The coins are held underneath two playing cards which are separated very slightly. These are held in the left hand.

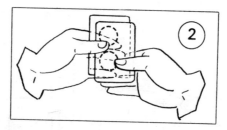

2. The right hand grasps the top card and at the same time, one coin is held by the right fingers under cover of the card.

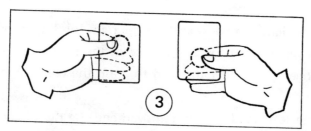

3. The right hand is now withdrawn with the hidden coin.

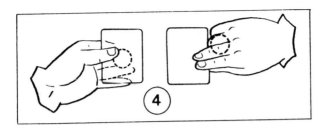

4. Right hand is now turned so that the back of the right hand is shown and the back of the card is shown while the coin is hidden by being finger palmed in the ring finger.

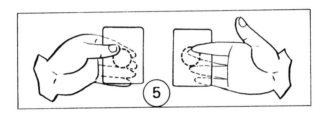

5. The right hand is turned with the palm open and the coin behind that card is held between the first and second finger.

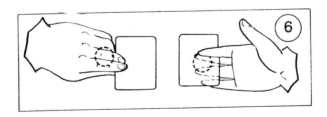

6. The left hand is turned over so that the back of that hand is shown and the coin is pulled into the left palm as the back of that card is seen.

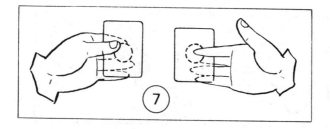

7. The left hand is returned to it's original position with the coin hidden by the playing card.

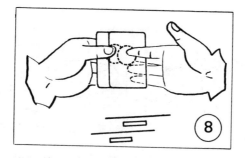

8. The two cards are held, still slightly separated. There is now a card and then a coin and then another card and under it another coin.

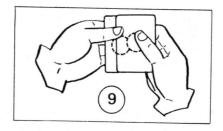

9. The right thumb is now brought to the top of the card.

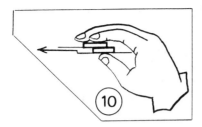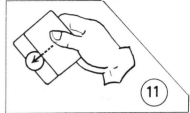

10. This is a special "top view" showing the right hand has turned over so that the thumb is on the bottom and the four fingers are on top of the two cards, hiding one of the coins.

11. While holding the coin with the right fingers, the pressure on the two cards is released and one coin is allowed to slide out from between the two cards and fall on to the table.

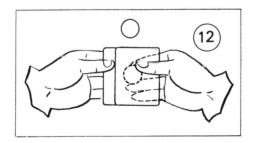

12. The right hand turns so that thumb is uppermost and the left hand now holds the bottom cards.

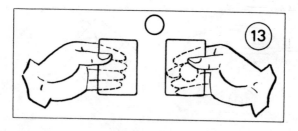

13. The left hand withdraws the bottom card to the left. Now one card is held in each hand.

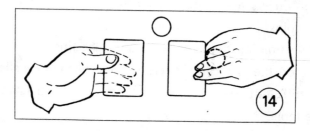

14. The right hand is again turned with the back of the hand uppermost and the coin under that card is pulled down into the right palm.

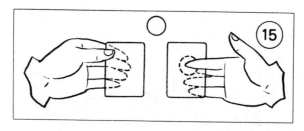

15. The right hand is turned back so that the right palm is shown to the audience and the coin is clipped between the first and second fingers as it is held behind the playing card.

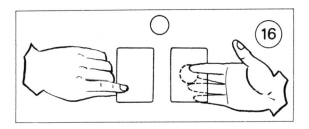

16. The left hand is turned over so that the back of that hand is shown along with the back of the card which is held in that hand.

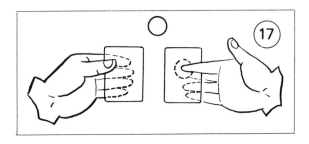

17. The left hand is turned back so that now the palm of the left hand is seen.

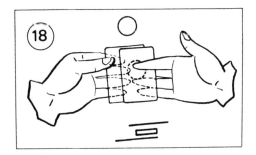

18. The two cards are brought together, although separated slightly, and the hidden coin is between them.

19. The right thumb now comes down to the top of the card.

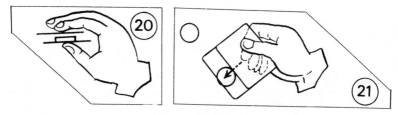

20. This is a "top view" showing the two cards and coin as they are held in the right hand.

21. Pressure is released on the two cards and the coin is allowed to slide down on to the table.

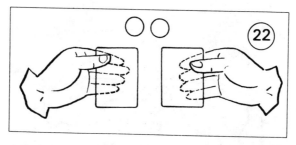

22. The left hand grasps the bottom card so that there is just one card in each hand and they are turned over together. The cards are put down on the table next to the coins as the hands are shown.

COINS PASSING THROUGH HANDKERCHIEF

EFFECT: Four coins are caused to pass through a handkerchief while the performer is seated at a table.

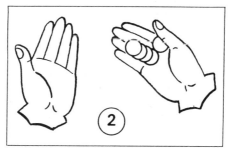

1. The handkerchief is spread out on the close-up pad
   which is on the table. On the right side of the table is a
   playing card and hidden in the performer's right coat
   pocket are five coins.

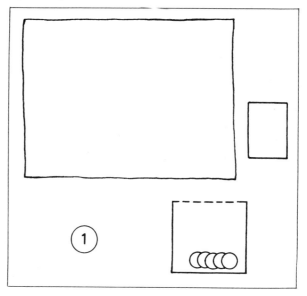

2. The right hand goes into the coat pocket, thumb palms
   one coin and brings out that coin and the other four
   coins.

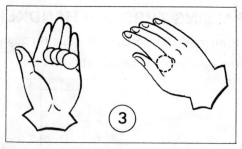

3. The right hand now drops the four coins into the left hand and they are shown to the audience.

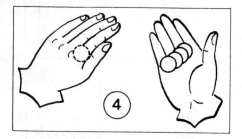

4. The left hand now thumb palms the coin which is resting closest to the left thumb. The three remaining coins are now dropped back into the right hand where they are assembled with the coin which had been thumb palmed by the right thumb.

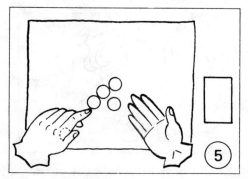

5. The coins in the right hand are now dropped upon the open handkerchief which is spread out upon the table.

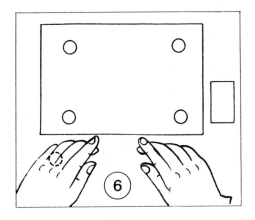

6. The four coins are palced near the four corners of the handkerchief and at the same time, the left hand changes the coin from the thumb palm to the finger palm position.

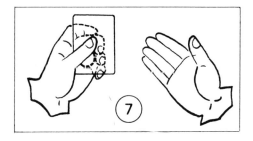

7. The right hand picks up the palying card and the card is passed to the left hand. The coin is hidden behind the card as the left palm is partially exposed to view.

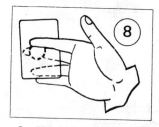 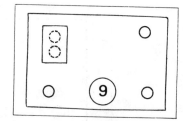

8. The right hand now clips the palying card between the right first and second fingers and at the same time, the coin behind the card is held by the first and second fingers.

9. The right hand now places the playing card over the coin which is resting at the upper left corner of the handkerchief. As the card is put down, the coin which had been hidden behind the card is also released and it remains with the other coin.

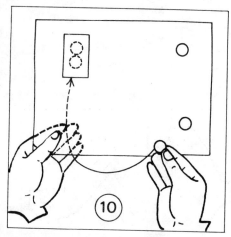

10. The right hand now picks up the coin which had been at the left bottom corner and the left hand lifts the left bottom corner of the handkerchief so that the right hand can be slipped under the handkerchief at that point.

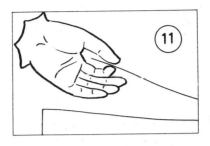

11. The handkerchief is held by the left thumb and forefinger and the other fingers of that hand are under the
handkerchief.

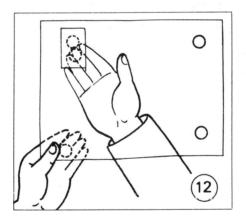

12. The right hand which is holding the coin now goes under
the handkerchief. The coin is secretly dropped on to the
three small fingers of the left hand as the right hand
continues on up under the handkerchief until it is
directly under the playing card which is resting at the
upper left corner.

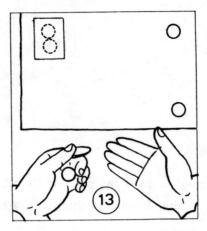

13. The right hand under the handkerchief makes a small movement as the performer explains that one coin is being passed through the handkerchief. The right hand is removed from under the handkerchief and it is shown to be empty. At the same time, the left hand has the coin finger palmed and it is brought away from the handkerchief.

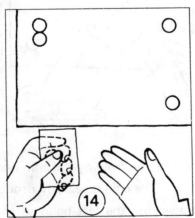

14. The right hand now lifts up the playing card and puts it into the left hand. The audience can now see the two coins.

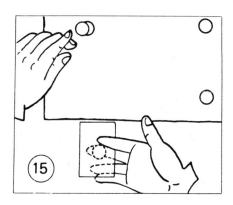

15. The left hand now passes the card with the coin hidden behind it to the right hand which receives the card and coin between the first and second fingers. The left hand then puts the two coins into a small pile.

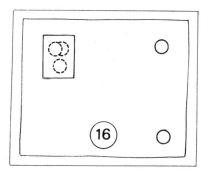

16. The playing card is now placed upon these two coins and at the same time, the hidden coin is placed on the handkerchief.

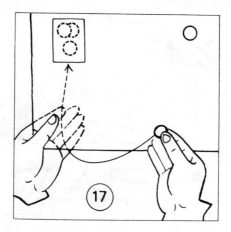

17. The right hand picks up the right bottom coin and the left hand picks up the left bottom corner of the handkerchief. This is exactly the same procedure as for the previous coin.

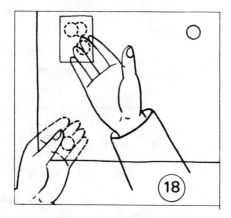

18. The right hand goes under the handkerchief and as it moves on it's way up towards where the playing card is resting, it first deposits the coin on the three small fingers of the left hand. When the right hand is in position under the card, it makes a small poking movement as the performer explains that the third coin is

being passed through the handkerchief to join the others.

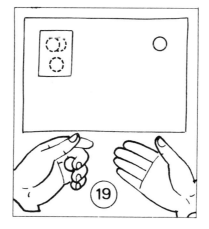

19. The empty right hand is now withdrawn from under the handkerchief and shown. At the same time, the left hand has the coin finger palmed and the left hand is withdrawn from the handkerchief.

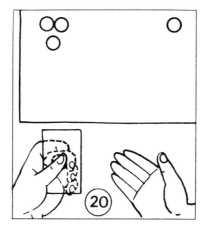

20. The right hand now picks up the playing card, showing the audience that the three coins are together. The card is put into the left hand where it is held to hide the coin which had been finger palmed in that hand.

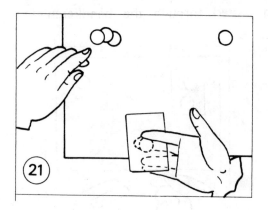

21. The left hand holds the card for a moment and then the playing card, together with the hidden coin, is passed to the right hand where the card and coin is clipped between the forefinger and middle finger as before. The left hand counts the three coins into a small stack and then spreads them apart so that they overlap slightly.

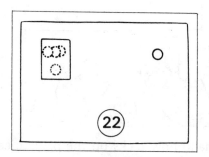

22. The playing card and the hidden coin is now placed upon the stack of three coins in the upper left corner.

23. The right hand now picks up the coin which has been in the upper right corner and at the same time, the left hand picks up the lower left corner of the handkerchief as before.

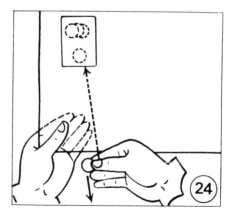

24. The right hand is now holding the coin and as it is about to pass under the left corner of the handkerchief the coin is deposited on top of the left knee.

For the beginner it is a good idea to have a napkin or handkerchief on the lap when performing this effect. This makes it easier to drop the coin into the lap with less chance that the coin might eventually drop to the floor.

If the performer is standing behind a table while performing this effect, it is still possible for him to deposit the fourth coin on the three small fingers of the left hand which then finger palms it as the left hand is withdrawn from the handkerchief. In this case, the left palm can not be shown.

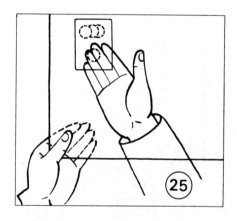

25. After the coin has been dropped into the lap or rested on the left knee, the right hand continues on up under the handkerchief until it is in position under the playing card.

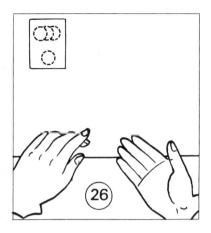

26. The right hand again makes a small movement under the handkerchief as he once again explains that the coin is being passed through the handkerchief to join the other coins under the card The right hand is slowly withdrawn from under the handkerchief and it is seen to be quite empty.

27. The right hand now picks up the playing card to show that all four coins have been assembled.

Gerald Kosky

Born on February 27, 1907 in Oil City, Pennsylvania. He has been active in various magic clubs in Los Angeles since 1925. Gerald Kosky is a past-president of the Pacific Coast Association of Magicians and a past national vice-president of the Society of American Magicians.

In 1977, Masatoshi Furota invited him to give several lectures to the magicians in Japan under the sponsorship of the Tenkai Awards Committee. His original ideas have been published in many books and magazines in the past forty seven years.

127 of his very best effects with cards and coins, along with his favorite mental effects have been compiled and published by Magic Limited in a huge 248 page book titled, "THE MAGIC OF GERALD KOSKY".

Ross Bertram

Born in Toronto, Canada in 1912, Ross Bertram has been performing as a magician and musician since his early school days. His background includes all types of performing from private parties and stage shows to trade conventions and performing on television.

His friendship with fellow Canadian, Dai Vernon, led to his traveling to New York City for the filming of some of his original tricks for The Stars of Magic.

During the Korean War, Ross Bertram entertained the Canadian troops in Japan and Korea. His fame has spread around the world.

"MAGIC AND METHODS OF ROSS BERTRAM" was published in 1978 by Magic Limited and it contains many excellent coin effects such as the Coin Thru Bottom Of Glass described on page sixteen of this book.

Ormond McGill

Born in 1913 in Palo Alto, California, He has toured the United States and Canada with a midnight spook show as Dr. Zomb. He traveled through India, The Philippine Islands and other countries of The Orient filming religious rites and temples.

Aside from his almost fifty years as an entertainer, his greatest contribution has been the large number of books he has written. Early works like "21 Gems of Magic" and "Atomic Magic" have become classics.

In his lectures and his program of "Mini-magic" he has always included his version of the Miser's Dream and Coins Across Into Glass that he has been featuring over the years in his stage show.

"ENTERTAINING WITH MAGIC" by Ormond Mcgill was published by A. S. Bernes and Co. in 1977 and it contains a fine chapter on simple coin tricks.

Jerry Andrus

Born in Sheridan, Wyoming in 1918, Jerry moved to Oregon as a young boy and has lived in Albany, Oregon for the past 45 years.

His various effects are always original in concept and in the methods used.

Since 1956 He has been lecturing throughout the United States and has been invited to lecture at magic convetions in England and Japan. Jerry Andrus was the first American Magician invited to tour Japan for Ton Onosaka and the Magicland Lecture Series.

He has written several books of original card tricks and his "MISER'S MIRACLE" contains fifty illustrations drawn by the author to cover all the details of the reputation making routine of producing several half dollar coins from under some entirely unprepared playing cards.

Pete Biro

Born on June 1, 1933 in Oakland, Calif. He began doing magic in High School and continued performing for the military throughout Europe following the Korean conflict.

When performing, Pete Biro is always thinking of entertainment first, usually with much originality. He performed for several years at The Magic Cellar in San Francisco and is very often seen at The Magic Castle in Hollywood. He has lectured extensively throughout the United States and at many National Magic Conventions.

He was extremely well received at the P.C.A.M. Convention which was held at The Imperial Hotel in Tokyo, Japan in 1977. He contributes a page of news and original ideas each month in the "S.O.B. Jr" magazine which is published by Lloyd E. Jones.

Daniel Cros

Born in Paris, France near Pigalle, in 1940, he became interested in magic while watching the street performers. At 15 he was a professional entertainer and at 16 he gave his first show at the famous Lido Cabaret.

He continued to perform at The Lido until 1964 when he came to Las Vegas to visit a friend and stayed on as a bartender-magician at the Monte Carlo Room of The Desert Inn Casino. The fact that he has been performing close-up magic at the same Desert Inn for the past fourteen years is a remarkable record and shows that he is indeed one of the finest magicians working in the fabulous entertainment capital of the world.

In 1977, Shigeo Futagawa arranged for Daniel Cros to visit Japan and present a series of lectures in Tokyo and Osaka for Ton Onosaka and the Magicland Concert Tour.

THE MAGIC OF TENKAI

Compiled and Edited by
Gerald Kosky
and
Arnold Furst

My Fifty
Years In Magic
by
Tenkai

Shigeo Futagawa

Limited Collector's Edition
Hardbound Fabricoid Cover
143 pages 8" x 11"
444 Drawings

Tenkai's autobiography, "My Fifty Years in Magic" plus over forty-five distinctive effects created by one of Japan's best loved magicians. Fully illustrated by Tenkai and Shigeo Futagawa and Bob Wagner.

$20.00
Plus 50c for postage

PUBLISHED BY MAGIC LIMITED, LLOYD E. JONES